Seriously Playful Magic

"Many people have the idea that magic is something that's deadly serious, if not somewhat sinister. They would find it hard to believe that there could be room for humor or frivolity. However, there's really a lot about magic that's playful. Magical thinking turns daily life into a world of enchantment. You can discover new wellsprings of energy, aliveness, spontaneity, and joy—the same qualities that are so much a part of children's play... This book is concerned both with perceiving the magic that's inherent in daily living, and in 'working magic' to help fulfill personal goals."

Magic is not separate from the routines of daily life—it permeates all existence. But the challenge is making magical philosophy work in the real world. How can you become a more playful, carefree person by integrating magical ideas into your lifestyle?

Janina Renee has written *Playful Magic* to give you an intriguing way to use metaphysical techniques and philosophies to enhance your daily life. The ideas, suggestions, and techniques described in this book offer effective, lighthearted, and fun ways to build positive energy. Anyone who wants to magically realign his or her thinking (including people who tend to find the idea of "magic" somewhat overwhelming or alarming) can successfully do so with the simple and enjoyable exercises in this book.

Let Janina Renee lead you along the playful path, where you will be encouraged to create your own magical fantasy realm, absorb yourself in the magical wonder of nature, imbue ordinary chores with magical purpose, achieve your personal goals, and enhance the quality of your life in many unforeseen ways.

About the Author

Janina Renee holds a degree in anthropology and is a scholar of such diverse subjects as folklore, ancient religions, mythology, magic, and psychology. She is particularly concerned with applying this knowledge to everyday life and is always looking for ways to translate the magic and mystery of the old ways into meaningful practices for modern people.

About the Artist

Alyn Gryphon is the son of the author, and was a high school freshman when he illustrated this book. He loves to draw and has created his own comic strips, board games, and concepts for video games. He has kept an illustrated dream diary since age 11, and has created a huge and detailed map of the landscapes of his dreams. His long-term goal is to become a genetic engineer in order to improve the conditions of humans and animals by stopping disease.

To Write to the Author

If you wish to contact the author or would like more information about this book, please write to the author in care of Llewellyn Worldwide, and we will forward your request. Both the author and the publisher appreciate hearing from you and learning of your enjoyment of this book and how it has helped you. Llewellyn Worldwide cannot guarantee that every letter written to the author can be answered, but all will be forwarded. Please write to:

Janina Renee
c/o Llewellyn Worldwide
P.O. Box 64383-678, St. Paul, MN 55164-0383, U.S.A.

Please enclose a self-addressed, stamped envelope for reply, or $1.00 to cover costs. If outside the U.S.A., enclose international postal reply coupon.

Free Catalog From Llewellyn

For more than 90 years, Llewellyn has brought its readers knowledge in the fields of metaphysics and human potential. Learn about the newest books in spiritual guidance, natural healing, astrology, occult philosophy, and more. Enjoy book reviews, New Age articles, a calendar of events, plus current advertised products and services. To get your free copy of *Llewellyn's New Worlds of Mind and Spirit,* send your name and address to:

Llewellyn's New Worlds of Mind and Spirit
P.O. Box 64383-678, St. Paul, MN 55164-0383, U.S.A.

Playful Magic

Janina Renee

1994
Llewellyn Publications
St. Paul, Minnesota 55164-0383, U.S.A.

FIRST EDITION
First Printing, 1994

Cover illustration: Denise Satter
Interior illustration: Alyn Gryphon, with an additional illustration by Thomas Fitch (p. 195).

Library of Congress Cataloging-in-Publication Data
Renee, Janina
    Playful magic / Janina Renee.
       p.   cm.
    Includes bibliographical references.
    ISBN 0-87542-678-6
    1. Magic.   2. Self-actualization (Psychology)   I. Title
BF1611.R455 1993   93-44559
133.4'3--dc20   CIP

Llewellyn Publications
A Division of Llewellyn Worldwide, Ltd.
P.O. Box 64383, St. Paul, MN 55164-0383

*This book is dedicated
to my parents.*

Acknowledgements

*I thank and acknowledge the contributions
of the following individuals...*

*Fred Adams, for his contributions
on Earth wisdom and enchantment...*

*Athena, who has shown me meaningful directions
with respect to Jungian studies and other knowledge
which has influenced the content of this book...*

*Ann, Beth, Daphne, Ed, Geoffrey, JoAnn,
Judy, Lorraine, Mara, Marion, Morgana, Pat,
Patricia, Shelly, Nancy, and Stephanie for sharing
insights into the nature of playful magic and
for providing a number of the anecdotes.*

Table of Contents

Introduction

I have long observed that good things happen more often to light-hearted people. They seem to be genuinely luckier, and all aspects of life just seem to work better for them. This made me realize that having a carefree, playful spirit can be the key to an enchanted existence. The playful spirit is a special quality of magic, and in magic there are lots of opportunities for playfulness.

Playful magic is born of creativity, spontaneity, intuition, joyfulness, and aliveness. It is both the producer and the product of that state known as "serendipity," where everything wondrously falls in place. It is best appreciated when the playful spirit in us experiences its relatedness to the playful spirit in Nature, as well as in our fellow beings. This book is devoted to exploring this special side of magic, and to offering some new insights into recovering the childlike sense of wonder which is its source. It applies these insights to creating goals, priming the pump for magic, understanding how your personality traits can open up new channels of influence and experience, creating magical fantasies, and sharing the magical energy of Nature and her denizens.

Playful Magic is also a how-to book that provides magical techniques for helping life run more smoothly. It offers affirmations, visualizations, meditations, spells, and magical techniques that are done in a spirit of fun and adventure. However, *Playful Magic* is more than just a spell book. It recognizes that magic isn't something that's separate from the routines of daily life—it's something that permeates all existence. To integrate magic into life is not to trivialize the deeper mysteries, but to make the mystery of living more meaningful.

We can see a subtle spirit of enchantment at work in everything, once we're open to it. *Playful Magic* looks for the magic inherent in things that are friendly and familiar, and shows you how to bring magic into everyday life in ways that are easy, natural, and meaningful. In fact, a lot of the "spells" and activities are built around the familiar functions of everyday life. You'll find that many of the things you may already do daily—such as work routines, crafts, and interactions with people—can be made playful and magical, just by looking at things differently. The techniques described herein are based on the idea that ordinary actions can be considered magical spells, and ordinary things can serve as material affirmations.

This unique magical philosophy can be especially helpful in getting us through hard times. Whether you are trying to get through an emotional depression or crisis, or are just trying to survive an economic recession, the playful approach enables you to divert yourself with pleasant and intriguing little magical goals and techniques. At the same time, you commend your security and desperation issues to the Higher Powers through a "Back Burner" spell before going "out to play," trusting that your Deity (or whatever you choose to call the intelligent process of the Universe) will provide for your most pressing personal needs. In this carefree approach, there is an underlying sense of spirituality, for it relies on the faith that the Higher Powers look after us as good parents look after their children, enabling the children to spend their time at play, which is truly children's work.

Expressing the playful Self brings spiritual and emotional enrichment, which includes nourishing the inner child. Many psychological and metaphysical systems emphasize that this child Self, or playful Self, is connected to our personal vitality, our intuition, and the unified state of mind and being that puts us in sync with the life pulse of the universe.

Since there's always a transformative element in experiencing or witnessing magic, this book can be useful to individuals who want to bring about deep personal changes, inner work, as well as individuals who want to make tangible changes in their material environment. It's an approach that helps people find creative ways to push the boundaries of their ordinary existence. Pursuing this playful path offers a form of self-betterment, and a form of therapy for spiritual, psychological, and physical healing.

Playful magic has a social and ecological ethic, for it emphasizes our relatedness to people and nature, and enables us to enter into a respectfully playful relationship with them.

People who might ordinarily be uninterested or intimidated by anything dealing with metaphysics will find the playful approach both appealing and accessible. It is a way to enrich daily life, infusing it with heart and meaning. You don't need any occult knowledge to enjoy the variety of suggestions and techniques offered here. Also, these magical workings are all about building good energy, so they do not lead to negative consequences.

Persons who already have developed interest and knowledge of the magical and metaphysical can find useful ideas in this book. *Playful Magic* provides observations and insights that are relevant and add wonder to any mystical philosophy or magical system.

Chapter 1

What Is
Playful Magic?

Playful Magic is a collection of meditations, visualizations, magical exercises, suggestions, and philosophy aimed at accomplishing nothing that's particularly important—nothing that you're desperate to achieve, nothing that your ego is riding on, nothing that your sense of security is relying on—only magical activities that are done "just for fun," or aimed at accomplishing only your more frivolous goals.

But why would anybody want to practice this playful magic? If you are going to get involved in some metaphysical practice, wouldn't you want to use it to solve your most pressing problems?

When we're beset by a lot of troubles, we tend to feel that we don't have time for any frivolities—but that's actually when we need them most. Most people turn to magic and mysticism when there is something they desperately desire but feel otherwise powerless to achieve. However, this is actually the worst time to expect magical success because desperation works against magic—it acts

1

as a negative affirmation. (See Appendix IV, for an explanation of the power and use of affirmations). Therefore, magic works better for people who don't worry about it, and wishes are more often granted to the people who are already happy and secure, rather than to the persons who seem to need them the most.

The practice of magic also calls for a special quality of energy, something which is also generated by playfulness. Energy is, after all, one of the main qualities of children and child's play. It goes hand in hand with joyfulness, aliveness, and pleasure.

Playfully Magical
Diversions

Playful magic is a collection of magical and fanciful diversions to take your mind off your most pressing concerns. The idea is that by engaging in these distractions, you hand your major life issues over to the care of your Higher Consciousness, or the Living Universe, or the Wide Ruling Powers, or your personal Deity, or whatever you choose to call it. This takes an element of faith, of course. It means trusting that your Life's Path will unfold before you just as it should. It's up to you to enjoy the journey, rather than hurrying worriedly towards an uncertain destination. You'll take care of the small things, and the bigger things will start falling into place.

The magical philosophy described here is designed to help you bring good things into your life, and have fun doing it. Magic of this type helps take us outside of ourselves and away from worries and problems. The philosophy and techniques of playful magic can show us the way to recover that special quality of energy which seems to be at the same time the source, the essence, and the product of playfulness—of being childlike, in all the best senses of the word.

Chapter 3 will help you define your personal magical goals, sorting them out into lists of the things you desperately feel you need, and the things that you would just "kind of" like to have. Then you can do things like visualizations and positive affirmations to achieve the objectives on the second list, the things you would "kind of" like—as well as taking physical actions that are devised as magical spells. For the not so important goals that are the target of playful magic, you can use some of the magical workings and techniques that are provided in the later chapters, or you can use some of the popular affirmations and visualizations or the more generalized manifestation techniques or spells to be found in various other New Age, metaphysical, and inspirational books, as there are quite a number of good ones available. Other goals to pursue while the Higher Powers are working on your personal issues include such broad aspirations as seeking rapport with Nature, gaining knowledge and enjoyment of your personal environment, and sharing good times with friends and family.

Of course, we can't just ignore our problems and our more pressing needs—that's too ingrained in human nature. To help set your mind more at ease, Chapter 3 also provides a little magical rite you can perform—a back burner spell. The Back Burner Spell lets you proclaim any special desires, the needs that may have a lot of desperation or ego riding on them. Then, you consign them to the Higher Powers to be taken care of while you concentrate on magical activities for fun and fulfillment.

Playful Can
Also Be Practical

Playful magic provides enjoyable, novel ways to work toward some of your goals and infuse your life with magic. You'll find that magical exercises performed with a sense of fun are likely to be the most successful. This type of magical philosophy will open up psychic potentials and new channels of power that will spill over into other areas of your life, making good things come to you more naturally. Serendipity, a happy-go-lucky state of being where the things you need or desire just seem to miraculously fall into your lap, can arise from your greater openness to joy and attunement to mystical currents. The playful approach to magic is also highly energizing; these lighthearted magical exercises will refresh and renew you. Playful energy is catching, you can be a "psychic battery," energizing other people without depleting yourself.

It almost goes without saying that this type of approach brings out the Inner Child, a psychological state a lot of people are trying to achieve these days. When you approach life light-heartedly, you develop a new mode of thinking and acting that includes seeing things in a new way (i.e., rediscovering that childlike sense of wonder), activating your creative potentials, pushing your life's boundaries, and being more spontaneous.

Other benefits that will follow naturally when you take a playful approach include:

- a cheerfulness, ebullience, and aliveness that will make you more radiant, more charming, healthier, and less stressed

- making life's fallow periods more interesting, bringing imagination, variety, and new modes of experience

- new levels of awareness, and the recognition that life can be savored in many different ways

- the greater extrasensory ability that comes with developing spontaneity and openness

- the deconditioning of instilled attitudes that it's wrong to spend time doing things just for fun and relaxation, or that it's wrong to work magic to benefit yourself

You may notice that many of the so-called magical spells and suggestions in this book border on some practical and therapeutic techniques for self-improvement, relieving stress, and exploring the inner self. Psychology and magic are really interrelated. Both involve entering the realm of dreams and possibilities, where fantasy affects reality and vice versa.

Can Magic Really Be Playful?

In keeping with the spirit of playful magic, I'm not going to make things complicated and serious by discussing all the different definitions of the word "magic," and the historical origins of all the various magical theories. To keep things simple, this book uses the term "magic" to denote anything that encourages us to feel that we can draw upon inner powers and weave subtle forces to shape desire and fantasy into reality. This book is concerned with both perceiving the magic that's inherent in daily living, and in "working" magic to help fulfill personal goals.

A lot of people have the idea that magic is something that's deadly serious, if not somewhat sinister. They would find it hard to believe that there could be room for humor or frivolity.

Part of this is due to a negative stereotype of magic users started during the Inquisition and perpetuated still by the media— you know, all those images of crazed people in black robes summoning demons and engaging in other activities that society frowns upon. Also, it often happens that when certain individuals first take an interest in and begin to explore the realms of psychism and magic, they often *do* take themselves very seriously, thereby contributing to either a heavy, grim, or loony image of the Occultist. This is especially true of less experienced or mature persons who are overly impressed with what a friend of mine calls "booga booga." These individuals can get a sense of power from freaking out their friends and family by acting and talking weirdly.

There is really a lot about magic that's playful. I'm not just talking about the tingly sensation we get in the presence of the mystical and otherworldly. Magical thinking turns daily life into a world of enchantment. By rediscovering your childlike sense of wonder, you can connect with the natural, spontaneous child in you. You

can look at things from new perspectives, seeing beauty and mystery in the ordinary things of life. You can discover new wellsprings of energy, aliveness, spontaneity, and joy—the same qualities that are so much a part of children's play.

Furthermore, to be a good magician, it has traditionally been held that you need to be open to perception and intuition so you can sense the ebb and flow of subtle tides of energy. You should be able to visualize your objectives and engage in other flights of fantasy. You have to overcome some inhibitions in order to do things that look strange or silly to other people. You are often called upon to think creatively. It is also important to be spontaneous enough to recognize and take advantage of magical opportunities. So, you see, the principles of traditional magic are not at all out of line with playful qualities and a light-hearted approach.

By the way, you will notice that there is nothing sinister or dangerous in the magical theories or exercises presented in this book, and nothing that is likely to have negative consequences. What's more, the spells and techniques are meant to be enjoyable and rewarding. You don't need to take them too seriously, and there's no need to be compulsive about following everything to the letter. Nothing baneful will happen if you don't do the magical workings exactly as suggested. And if you are unable to complete a magical working, it's no big deal. You can still expect to get a lot of good effects from the good energy you'll have started in motion.

Ethics

Our experimentation with amusing new ways to explore magic does have some limitations. Out of a sense of ethics, consideration for others, and for fear of negative psychic repercussions, there are some things that we don't want to play around with. Should you decide to go deeper into magical research and experimentation, use good judgment in evaluating the sort of material you might come across and the ways you might be tempted to use it.

Keep in mind the following:

- Don't toy with other people's emotions. Love spells that aim to control other people's wills are bad medicine. (Although there's nothing wrong with using a little magic to enhance the pleasure of an already existing love relationship.)

- Avoid the temptation to use mystical knowledge to play tricks or mind games.

- Don't use magic for petty revenge or practical joke spells. That kind of humor is tainted and will shut you off from the inner wellsprings of magical energy that playful magic seeks to open up.

Basically, steer clear of any magical actions designed to exert power over other people, and any sort of mean-spiritedness. There's nothing trite about the saying, "Do unto others as you would have them do unto you."

There is a tendency for some people to view the practice of magic as being innately unethical. Some of this stems from religious views which see anything that is not condoned by their religion as being evil. There's also some concern that some magic workers might harm other people. In response to the former, no amount of persuasion can change the minds of people who want to project evil into everything. In answer to the latter, it's true there are unethical people in the world, but experience has shown that competent practitioners of black magic are very rare, and the ones that exist are too preoccupied with their personal problems to go about casting spells on neighbors, relatives, and random strangers. Most of them are immature people who don't have the native ability or diligence to stick with any metaphysical disciplines because they don't produce the fast and spectacular results they are seeking. You will also notice that playful magic does not lend itself to negative or manipulative magic, and the sense of wholeness and security that comes from the playful attitude is a good shield against bad vibes, regardless of their sources.

Additionally, there are some individuals who have a world view of "limited good." They feel that there is only a finite amount of good luck in the world, so if someone gains some kind of benefit in one area, someone else is going to have to lose out on something somewhere else. Such an attitude is totally at odds with New Age beliefs. Good luck and prosperity are infinitely expandable. Look at it this way: if you exercise to build up your muscles, it does not mean that someone somewhere else is going to experience a corresponding loss of muscle mass. So it is possible for one person's good to increase without diminishing that of another. Playful magic is in keeping with this expansive philosophy.

Chapter 2

Setting Out on the Playful Path

Before we get down to the actual magical suggestions and techniques, it's important to look at the attitudes and qualities that can enable you to become a natural conduit of playful magic. After all, you can be greatly enriched by making the playful spirit a part of your lifestyle.

Spontaneity is a highly magical mode that means being free-spirited, flexible, open-minded, and receptive to impulses,[1] feelings, senses, and perceptions. This is a state of being and acting that can open many channels of opportunity and enchantment. For the person who would like to become attuned to the tides of mystical power, a part of spontaneity is seizing magical opportunities. This book provides some ideas for magical fun, and experiencing these things will encourage new ideas to come to you automatically. Let your intuition guide you in learning how to be spontaneous. Become sensitive to urges, even if they seem a little kooky. If an idea for something unique and interesting to do pops into your head or comes up in one of your dreams—do it as soon as possible!

Spontaneity also involves allowing yourself to be led by your curiosity. This is another important aspect of playfulness—it's one of the qualities of the natural child. When you have new things you want to explore, learn more about, try, or have new things to discover, you renew yourself and generate energy and enthusiasm. Let your curiosity take you in new directions. For example, if you tend to be an extroverted person, let your curiosity lead you to explore your inner world. Or, if you have been mainly inwardly focused, find interests that will help you venture outward.

In achieving spontaneous qualities and indulging your natural curiosity, you can learn to enter into a state of timelessness. To get into the spirit of playful magic, you have to be willing to take the time to do some frivolous things. It's important to have periods when you're not being affected by time pressures, because these stifle your natural energy and creativity. Playfulness, creativity, and energy are all interrelated. Friedrich Schiller felt that play is the expression of exuberant energy; he credited play as the origin of all art.[2] It's necessary to have time set aside when you give yourself permission to play games, goof off, or lie around and do nothing, as well as time to devote to hobbies or concentrate on your inner psychic and spiritual life without worrying about your other concerns.

Since engaging in play and playfully magical activities will energize you and stimulate the Life Force flowing through you, it's especially good if you can arrange to do some fun things first thing in the morning, before you get on to other work. If you feel guilty because your work is piling up and you just can't justify spending time on yourself, remind yourself that indulging your curiosity will open up an inner wellspring of energy. Your increased vitality will enable you to bring more enthusiasm and focus to your work life, improving its quality and quantity. Dr. Paul Pearsall lists "the savoring of the moments of life that are all too often missed" as part of his prescription for superjoy. He points out, "If we wait for

everything we want accomplished to be completed before we celebrate, we will miss the party of life."[3] So by all means, make fun a
priority. Reserve a place for it in your schedule and allow it to
interrupt your schedule sometimes.

A playful attitude will enable you to take things as they come,
experience the ebb and flow of life's tides, and just allow life to
happen without trying to over-manage everything. When problems arise, you see them as part of the natural flow, rather than as
interruptions and obstacles to it. You learn to take better advantage
of the playful opportunities and experiences life offers you.

Humor is essential for getting into the spirit and finding the
enchantment we seek. People generally don't think of humor and
magic as the sort of things that traditionally go together. It's common to think of magic as being something solemn and serious.
However, in *The Spiral Dance,* Starhawk emphasizes that humor
and play awaken the sense of wonder. She says, "The sense of
humor, of play, is often the key to opening the deepest states of
consciousness."[4] We can also see a gentle appreciation of humor
when Amber Wolfe discusses her shamanic insights and experiences in *In the Shadow of the Shaman.*[5]

The connection between the playful self and inner wellsprings
of power and magic is increasingly being recognized and recommended by the metaphysical community. In *The Candle Magic
Workbook,*[6] Kala and Katz Pajeon suggest that by embracing "the
Child Self" you will find:

> Your life suddenly becomes smoother and calmer. When you
> have questions in life, answers seem to come from nowhere.
> You find your ESP increasing. There is an inner attitude
> change taking place. Knowledge you did not know you pos-
> sessed surfaces. And, best of all, you have just gained years
> on most practitioners of magick. This is a truth that few real-
> ize. Your Child Self is the key to extrasensory perception, to
> obtaining the proper energies you require to manifest magick
> into your life.

The playful person knows how to look at things from unique perspectives. Notice how children have a tendency to look at things: standing on their heads, bending over and looking through their legs, crawling under beds and tables, climbing on top of things, peeking through holes and into crevices, etc. Seeing things from different angles increases our appreciation of them. It enables us to see beauty and wonder in the everyday aspects of life, even in the smallest details. We develop an ability to see details we don't ordinarily notice: textures, structures, lines, shapes, sounds, smells, and so on. The ability to perceive and handle things differently and unconventionally also facilitates creativity, artistry, and invention. Working playful magic enables you to more fully develop all of the these qualities, especially if you feel you are weak in any of them.

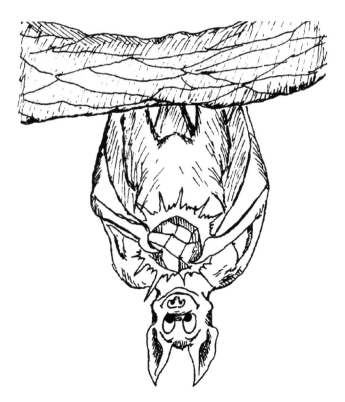

Bringing Magic into Life

When we invoke and enhance the playful qualities previously discussed, there are a number of ways we can see them spilling over into daily life. We develop magical ways of seeing and acting.

A playful attitude is often accompanied by a tendency to see the world of Nature and things around us, including inanimate objects, as having a life of their own. Perhaps because we are celebrating our own aliveness, we learn to celebrate life in all things. We can see ourselves as having a relationship with these objects: interacting with them, appreciating them, respecting them, and playing with them in a good-natured manner.

The little things the playful person does reflects this attitude—things like greeting your coffee pot, thanking your chair for its comfort, welcoming a sunbeam, or throwing a kiss to the Moon. The idea that there is a spark of the sacred even in inanimate objects and everyday things is part of a world view that sees all life and all matter as being connected. This is a philosophy called "animism." Maeterlink's children's story *The Bluebird,* which has been made into two movies, illustrates this belief. Things like milk, sugar, water, and light are shown as living beings having their own personalities.

My friend Lorraine Jr. was raised by a mother who taught her that there is nothing you can touch, do, or think that is not magic, and this included an animistic outlook. Lorraine says that "the reality is the magic." With this, there is a great awareness and respect for life because "everything has a say-so and a count."

Fantasy is an important part of playfulness, and an appreciation of fantasy enables a person to bend reality in playful ways. An ability to indulge in fantasies does not necessarily imply believing in every popular delusion, but the capacity for imaging often acts as a gateway for opening dormant senses and stimulating intuition.

Notice how readily and instinctively children take to fantasy. I think most children, even while still relatively young, are generally aware of the difference between fantasy and reality. However, they embrace fantasy and go along with pretense anyway, because they are intuitive enough to know that fantasy gives you a glimpse of the numinous realms. Thus, a child may be sophisticated enough to know, or at least to suspect, that there's no Santa Claus, but he or she enjoys being carried along with the fantasy. So have fun pretending you are persons or things that you're not, and you will discover new facets of your personality. Pretend that there is hidden beauty and goodness in situations and things that really look grim, and you might find that things turn out better than expected. Act as if there are angels and elves, and maybe you'll find that there are angels and elves.

Behaving playfully and acting out magical fantasies have valid psychological and physiological benefits. It is common to think that our moods dictate our behavior. However, scientists have found that it can also work the other way around; certain behaviors can induce certain moods. For example, if you force yourself to smile, even if you don't really feel happy, the contraction of muscles and other physiological mechanisms involved in the action of smiling increase the flow of blood and oxygen to the brain and release chemicals that alter your psychological state, making you feel happier.

Dr. Paul Pearsall emphasizes this capacity of mood to follow behavior in *Super Joy,* recommending, "the actual saying of joy words can help produce the psychochemical changes that are the healthy drugs to which we hope to be addicted." He adds, "Motivation is also preceded by behavior, and just as you must force yourself to get up, get dressed, and go out for a brisk early morning walk, so must you start thinking and behaving joyfully before you really feel like it."[7] You can see the implications of this concept: if we engage in playful activities, we really will feel more carefree, and if we engage in magical fantasies, we can experience that tingly feeling that comes when we are in the presence of greater mysteries.

Pushing Your Boundaries

In order to be spontaneous, experience new things, look at things from different perspectives, open new channels of opportunity, and discover new worlds of adventure, it is necessary to extend your boundaries.

The boundaries which define the limits of your life experience can include the geographical area you move around in, the people you associate with, the level of your education, your daily work routine, even the way you entertain yourself—if you find that your ordinary recreational activities are too limiting or repetitious. It follows that you can extend those boundaries by getting out and exploring new areas, learning new things, being willing to make sudden and spontaneous changes in your routine, and looking for fun in new types of activities.

Meeting and dealing with different types of people is a very significant way to push your boundaries. Make a point of getting to know people who have different types of knowledge and experience than the people you normally associate with, including younger people, older people, and people of different sexes, races, religions, and classes.

You can change your outlook by trying to do things in slightly different ways. If you are right-handed, you may bear to the right when you go places and do things, walking with your right side to the shops, and houses to get the best view. Try doing the reverse and bearing to the left, or vice versa if you're left-handed.

The playful approach to magic can provide additional ways to push those boundaries. Some of the suggestions in the following chapters will touch on this, and in the course of developing spontaneity, additional ideas will occur to you. Of course, just the fact that you're willing to explore things magical and fanciful means that you are already going outside the boundaries of what is usual in our society.

Crossing the borders of our knowledge and experience can put us in contact with the "inferior functions" of ourselves and society, which can open the gates to inspiring realms of psychic and psychological experience. (See Chapter 4 for an explanation of inferior functions.) This can bring us into the company of a forgotten Archetype; the Divine Maiden, known as the Kore or the Star Maiden, who is a personification of the playful Spirit of Nature. According to Frederick McLaren Adams, founder of Feraferia, a group dedicated to celebrating Wilderness and restoring the vitality of Earth's sacred places:

> The Divine Maiden is the "inferior function" of the Global Monoculture. She emanates a loving spirit of service in the mode of profound levity and sublime playfulness. Our culture is characterized by a fatal split: "beastly seriousness" on the one hand and "trivial pursuits" on the other. Between these there seems to be no middle ground. But the archetypal sphere of the Maiden lies precisely in this *terra incognita.*[8]

"Boundaries" can also include instilled attitudes and restraints on behavior and emotions. Such limitations stifle our joy, our aliveness. Here again, the playful approach can help, and we can emulate children in order to learn new ways. Children express their emotions freely, they sing, laugh, and cry when they feel like it, they don't worry about how they look or what other people are thinking. When children engage in play, they have no qualms about acting weird, silly, or wild. Seemingly foolish behavior serves the creative needs of the right brain hemisphere. I know that whenever I do dumb things, I catch a lot of mental flak for these silly embarrassments. However, it helps to remind your inner critic that embarrassment is a risk worth taking. To be afraid to let your hair down and make a fool of yourself is to cut off the voice of the

right brain, thereby cutting yourself off from a great store of riches.

If you find that you are putting off or are reluctant to try an activity that will take you out of your boundaries, ask yourself whether it is dangerous or costly. If not, then inertia is probably the problem. For example, when I'm intellectualizing about things like I am right now while I am writing this book, the idea of stimulating magical channels by going out and around to interesting places seems very exciting. However, it's too easy to fall into complacency. When there's something going on in town such as a craft show or lecture, on the day in question, I often don't feel like going out. I don't want to interrupt my work schedule or tear myself away from projects I'm involved in. But that's the very reason it is necessary to break out of routine from time to time. One way to get around this is through planning. By committing yourself in advance to going somewhere, you can get psyched up for it. However, spontaneity needs to be developed too. It's good to learn to pick up and go somewhere without advance thought—just to help you learn where the flow of energy is leading.

Pushing boundaries and following the flow of energy puts you in rapport with another very playful archetype, best known as Mercury or Hermes, messenger and mediator of the gods, guide of souls, "Bringer of Luck," patron of creativity and inspiration, and god of boundaries. He is also the archetypal Trickster, and when a person is acting in accordance with the true purpose of the Self, the Trickster can be the friendliest of the gods, acting as a catalyst to make happy and lucky coincidences happen. Combs and Holland especially emphasize this role of the Trickster and the importance of being open to energy flow and outcome:

> Adopting a playful mood toward synchronicity means following the Trickster wherever he leads, knowing that we are led by the guide of souls. It means to lighten up—to pay attention to where the flow of coincidence leads. In doing so, we honor the Trickster.[9]

We humans tend to get locked into our routines, and it's hard to expend the energy necessary to try to do something in a new and different way. Perhaps the main thing to remember here is that by expending energy, we invite magic, we generate a new quality of energy and experience, as well as many other benefits.

Your Life
Path

All of us are concerned about being on the right path in life, "the path with heart."[10] When an individual starts to follow the course that is right for himself or herself, everything else is more likely to fall into place. Magical, wonderful, synchronous, serendipitous events will smooth the way. That's why it is important to feel comfortable in the knowledge that the things you want are right for you. Marcus Bach, whose writings are concerned with the subject of serendipity, says:

> One of the secrets is to believe that a good fate is on our side, that the deepest longings of the heart have a special meaning or they would not have arisen within us in the first place.[11]

Bearing Bach's quote in mind can prevent a lifetime of guilt and anxiety from repressing your longings because they seem impractical or self-indulgent. Having a playfully magical approach to life can also help you find your path. If you're experiencing indecision and uncertainty about whether you're taking the right course in life, try lightening things up. Relieving stress with playful diversions will enable you to be more open and perceptive SO YOUR PATH CAN FIND YOU. Remember the story of Peter Pan. Peter could always find his way back to Neverland, because Neverland would always come looking for him!

Getting Around
Obstacles

You will find that taking on the playful magical philosophy will help you push your boundaries, develop new and positive attitudes and habits, and overcome a lot of obstacles. However, you may encounter some resistance from social or environmental circumstances or old attitudes. When you try to get into the spontaneous, magical mindset to work these spells and try out these suggestions, consider whether some of the following problems apply.

If, in trying to engage your sense of curiosity and wonder, you find that there's nothing new that you would like to do or learn, it's probably because you long ago cut yourself off from some of your innermost sources of joy, your inner needs and desires.[12] You probably shoved these things aside because you felt that you had to concentrate on work and all of your other obligations, and you just couldn't justify spending time nonproductively. Now is the time to break those old patterns and rediscover the naturally inquisitive and adventurous child inside of you. If you must, work at finding things that interest you. Probe deeply into the past, try to recall things that excited your interest when you were younger.

Also, you might find yourself locked into certain social or environmental circumstances which prevent you from freely exploring and expressing your own interests. If you can't indulge your natural creativity and spontaneity because your physical circumstances are too restrictive, take both physical and magical actions to either rearrange your environment or get yourself into a new set of circumstances that are more congenial to your needs. I am not able to go into detail about how to do this here, as that would be the subject of another book. Also, this is a matter where each individual has to find his or her own way. However, I will say that sometimes you have to break out of a bad place through a series of small steps: upgrading your education and job skills, moving into new social circles, analyzing which of your own attitudes are holding you back, and so on. Then again, sometimes you have to take drastic steps, even if it means leaving a home or a way of life that is safe and familiar. Motivational speaker Les Brown is fond of saying words to this effect, "No one ever learned to swim by standing on the shore. You just have to plunge into the water."[13] I hope some of the suggestions and techniques in *Playful Magic* will actually help you with some of those steps, whether large or small.

It was mentioned earlier that learning to listen to and trust your intuition goes hand in hand with developing the spontaneity necessary for a serendipitous, magical lifestyle. In the course of growing up in our society—and this is particularly true in dysfunctional families—there are a lot of forces that train us to shut off our internal information systems. I think the best way to counteract this is to make a conscious effort to listen to your inner voices, then act on them whenever you can. You can start by doing this in very small ways. If you're suddenly seized by a desire to go draw circles in the sand (and you don't live too far from a beach), then hop to it! This shows your Higher Consciousness that you're receptive to its advice, so you will be more likely to be the recipient of further inspiration. When we start following our intuition on things, it may at first seem like nothing is coming of it. For example, we may be inspired to take some action or go to some place, only to find that nothing meaningful or eventful happens to us there (or at least not as far as we can see). However, we have to realize that we need to make up for long years of distrust. Most of us are so far out of attunement, we will need a lot more practice at acting on trust. Fortunately, it's easier to listen to your intuition and build confidence in it when you are in the playful mode.

Certain people, whether by nature or due to certain types of religious or social training, feel awkward about the idea of seeking magical rewards for themselves. Many have a notion that it's either selfish or improper to ask for something for yourself. Of course, you need to decondition yourself from this type of thinking. More and more often people today are coming to realize that we have to love and take care of ourselves in order to live full lives, and to be able to help others. Because this awareness has become so strong, there are now a lot of books, seminars, and therapies available on how to look to your own needs. I particularly recommend the teachings of Louise L. Hay regarding these matters.[14]

Reordering
Your Life

One of the classical principles of magic is that by acting on things in the outer, physical world we can affect changes in our inner beings, and that by undergoing transformations in our internal, mental and spiritual life, we can change the our material world. This is based on the belief that the inner and outer are interlinked, or mirrors of each other, and that change in one area automatically brings some form of change or movement in the other area. Thus, if you want to make changes in your external circumstances, such as job, relationships, environment, and level of prosperity, you can help things along by devoting time to activities that are mentally and spiritually enriching such as religious practice, meditation, spiritual retreats and seminars, reading, therapy, etc. If inner work happens to be one of your personal goals, one of the ways you can get a start on it is by making changes in your exterior conditions. As mentioned above, sometimes you have to break out of restrictive circumstances, whether by taking drastic action or by taking a series of small steps. The added benefit is that whatever you accomplish externally will also bring inner growth and change.

Endnotes

1. Please be aware that in encouraging impulsiveness, we still have to be guided by common sense and our responsibility to do right by the other people in our lives. Don't do anything that might jeopardize your safety, your livelihood, or your relationships.

2. It's interesting to note that most of the world's creative inspirations and inventions are born in "stew-around time"—time that is not consciously focused on achieving anything in particular.

3. Pearsall, Paul, Ph.D. *Super Joy.* New York: Doubleday, 1988. Page 61.

4. Starhawk. *The Spiral Dance.* San Francisco: Harper and Row, 1979.

5. Wolfe, Amber. *In the Shadow of the Shaman*. St. Paul: Llewellyn, 1988.

6. Pajeon, Kala and Katz. *The Candle Magic Workbook*. New York: Carol Publishing Group, 1991. Page 51.

7. Pearsall, Paul, Ph.D. *Super Joy*. New York: Doubleday, 1988. Pages 17 and 34.

8. Frederick McLaren Adams, April 17, 1992, personal correspondence.

9. Combs, Allan, and Holland, Mark. *Synchronicity—Science, Myth, and the Trickster*. New York: Paragon House, 1990. Page 135.

10. The term "path with heart" was introduced by Carlos Castaneda in *The Teachings of Don Juan: A Yaqui Way of Knowledge* (San Francisco: Harper and Row, 1968) and explored further by Jean Bolen in *The Tao of Psychology* (San Francisco: Harper and Row, 1979).

11. Bach, Marcus. *The Wonderful Magic of Living* (Garden City: Doubleday, 1986). Another of his books which seems to be a companion to this is *The World of Serendipity* (Marina Del Ray: DeVorss, 1970).

12. It may also be a symptom of depression. If this applies to you, get help. If you try to cure depression by yourself, it may take you years. However, in combination with proper therapy, finding pursuits that engage your curiosity can be very effective in turning depression around.

13. As remembered from a speech heard at Unity (Warren, Michigan), summer of 1990.

14. Hay, Louise L. *You Can Heal Your Life*. Santa Monica: Hay House, 1984.

Chapter 3

Setting Magical Goals

The word "magic" tends to be used in two different senses. In one sense, it refers to that which is numinous, anything that evokes our sense of wonder and enables us to feel connected to deeper mysteries. In the other sense, we talk about "working magic," which involves shaping subtle, mystical energies to help us achieve certain personal goals. Having a playful attitude can enable us to connect with our childlike enjoyment of wonder, giving us new perspectives, enabling us to see and touch the magical mysteries inherent in living, and infusing daily life with enchantment. However, we can also take a playful approach to goal-oriented magic.

One way to get a good start on working toward your magical objectives is to define them and sort them out. When you want to say affirmations,[1] cast spells, or use other magical techniques, it obviously helps to have some kind of object in mind. For the purposes of playful magic, the most frivolous goals are the ones that are best to get started first.

To begin, make a long and generalized list of things you'd like to have. Put down anything that comes to your mind, anything at all, no matter how major or minor, no matter how far out or seemingly impossible. Don't just put down things that you badly want, put down things that you would kind of like to have as well. You can probably think of a broad range of material items to put on your wish list. They can be big and expensive, such as a mansion on your own Caribbean island, or small and common, like a new floor mat or potato peeler. You can list certain types of benefits such as new jobs, promotions, business and social opportunities, even love entering your life. It's also appropriate to list things you would like to do, such as trips you would like to take, skills you would like to learn, people you would like to see, as well as personal qualities, achievements, and improvement goals like losing weight, developing charisma, being a better listener, improving health, etc. Generalized desires such as increased prosperity, more satisfying relationships, changes for the better, and so on, can be listed too, so you cover all the bases.

Work on your list over a period of several days, as you will be continuously thinking of new things to add. The longer the list, the better. You might eventually want to sort out your goals and desires into different categories, and you can try writing them down using different color inks to give yourself a better visual appreciation of your lists.

When you've got a pretty full list, go through it and put some kind of mark next to any items that you want so badly you can taste it, anything that evokes a sense of desperation or urgency, or strong ego attachment. Now, separate your entries out into two new lists. Put the desperation and ego items that you marked off on a special list, which can be used in the following Back Burner spell. The second list can consist of everything that's left. We'll refer to this as the secondary list, or the "kind of would like to have" list. These goals don't have a strong negative emotional charge on them, so they can be used for playful magic. (However, you can be creative about finding ways to use secondary goals that are in support of primary goals, as long as you are able to keep them detached from desperate emotions.)

Some of the following chapters provide light-hearted magical visualizations, spells, and creative techniques that you can experiment with to work toward manifesting some of the things on your secondary wish list. You may be able to attract some of the desired items by performing the Good Things Coming In spell provided in Chapter 8, the perpetual spells in Chapter 9, or through the use of fantasy, crafts, and toys as detailed in Chapters 6, 10, and 11.

You may enjoy looking into other books offering techniques for manifesting desired goals through visualizations and affirmations, or spell books and magical manuals for techniques to try out with these particular goals, as there are a very wide and fascinating variety in print. Naturally, I highly recommend my book *Tarot Spells,* which has 71 different spells to choose from, including such potentially playful subjects as action, artistic and creative concerns, beauty, health and fitness, change, dreams, friends, emotions, knowledge, luck, motivation, psychism, and self-improvement.2 You can also work toward the things on your secondary list by consulting manuals on candle burning, use of talismans and charms, color, crystals, rune lore, techniques of natural magic, and many other methods for working on goals that range from the physical to the spiritual, the mundane to the otherworldly. For items on the list of more desperately desired things, consider doing the following magical rite.

Back Burner Spell

The Back Burner spell encourages you to trust the process of Life. When you give your larger set of cares over to the Higher Powers, you can then put your energies into taking care of the needs of the minute, as well as permitting yourself some playful goals, opportunities, and diversions.3

However, I do want to emphasize that doing the Back Burner spell doesn't mean you then neglect the big issues, you just don't give them all of your emotional energy. For example, if you need to get a job, this is certainly a desperation issue for most of us. To do this in the spirit of playful magic, you would address the Higher Powers, calling their attention to your need in some form of ritual, such as the Back Burner spell. Then, put in a reasonable number of hours each day doing the necessary things such as checking ads, sending out résumés, etc. When you've finished your day's session of job hunting, you would then disassociate yourself from it, don't worry about it, don't even think about it, but turn your attention to activities that nourish you. And if you feel like working some magic, direct your magical energy toward the secondary things or the playful things, since you accept that the job issue is now already being magically worked on by the Higher Powers.

The Back Burner spell is a way of consigning your desperation items and seemingly impossible dreams to the keeping of the Universe. Think of the Higher Powers as good parents who attend to their children's basic needs by providing comfort and security, taking care of the cooking, cleaning, mending of clothes, etc. This frees the kids to do the job they need to do, which is not merely learning but also playing. Yes, playing can be considered to be children's work. Play serves important functions, enabling children to explore their environment, develop a relationship with their world, and work out their feelings. Play is also a natural expression of the Life Force, into which children seem to have an open pipeline. We could all benefit by tapping into this pipeline more readily.

In order to perform the Back Burner spell, it's necessary to make a list of the things you most desperately want and which seem most difficult to obtain, as mentioned above; this is your "back burner list." Keep this list separate from the list of things which you merely would like and which are generally not so difficult to get, which is your secondary list. When you've decided you want to perform the Back Burner spell, take the following steps:

1. Make plans to go somewhere that's fun and interesting, such as a movie, park, museum—whatever happens to appeal to you. This is a very important part of the spell, so don't try to skip this part, do whatever it takes to work your outing into your busy schedule.

2. Shortly before you leave on your outing, get out your back burner list. Get a new piece of paper and make yet a new list by rewriting the items on your back burner list, phrased as positive affirmations, which is to say, expressed as if these things had already come true. Write your affirmations in the present tense, avoiding future tense words such as "will have" or "shall be." For example: "I have lots and lots of money." "I adore my beautiful house and sprawling acreage in the country." "I enjoy taking frequent trips to Hawaii." If you're not used to writing affirmations, these might seem like outrageous lies, but you must

accept that there's a magical principle that when you say a thing is true it is true. It may be that for the moment it's only true, within a certain plane of reality, but that other plane of reality holds the forms and templates for our own physical reality.

Make the writing of this list and its translation into affirmations into a little ritual. First, have prepared a ritual space that will allow you to focus completely on rewriting your list by setting aside a time and place where you can be free of distractions. Lay your materials out on a table, which you can enhance by decorating with colored cloths, fresh flowers, and crystals and gemstones (see Appendix II on color symbolism you can use for all of the afore-mentioned decorations). To help create additional ambience and focus, you may also wish to have a candle lit while you make your list (see Appendix I on how to prepare candles for magical pur-poses), burn incense, and play classical or New Age music or any of your favorite musical pieces. Have pen and paper ready too, so you can prepare your list of affirmations.

If you like, you can begin the rite by doing a little invocation to announce your desire to commit your concerns to the Higher Pow-ers. (You can name your deity instead of using the terms Living Universe or Higher Powers.) To do this, put your hands over the blank paper in an attitude of blessing, and say something like:

> *I give my concerns to the keeping*
> *of the Living Universe.*
> *I am ready to receive*
> *all of the qualities and all of the things*
> *that I now write on this list.*
> *All of these things are good for me.*
> *All of these things are right for me.*
> *I accept that the Higher Powers have*
> *already prepared these things for me.*
> *I am ready to receive my good,*
> *and it is already here for me!*

Now, as you sit down and begin to rephrase your desires as affirmations and put them down on paper, say each affirmation aloud as you write it down. When you feel that your list is com-plete and you've made your last affirmation, you can close the rite by saying something like:

I have completed my list,
        at least for the time being.
I know I can always change it
        or add to it if I want to.
I accept that the Higher Powers are taking care of
        my needs, and I am now ready to have fun.
I welcome life's rich experiences.
I open myself to joy and wonder.
I open myself to all the opportunities offered to me.
And now I'm going out to play!

Extinguish any candles, and put the list of affirmations into an envelope. Any color envelope, including ordinary white, is fine, but a red envelope is especially recommended. Red is the color of activity, and symbolizes your wishes being actively brought to birth. Red envelopes can commonly be found in some Christmas card boxes. Red is also considered to be very lucky in China and certain other Asian countries, some of whose peoples give gifts of money sealed in small red envelopes imprinted with good luck symbols as part of their New Year's celebration. If you can obtain such an envelope, that would be a particularly nice touch. If you wish, you can also include religious icons or good luck symbols in the envelope with your affirmations.

If you want to keep your list, you can leave the envelope in a special place in your home, such as on your dresser, in a drawer, a memorabilia box, or your personal files. The advantage of keeping the list is that from time to time you can review it and revise it, adding new items and hopefully even crossing out some things that actually come to pass. (You may want to add a star, smiling face, or other acknowledgment of fulfillment whenever you cross something off.) It's always fascinating to look at old lists, not merely to see which of your desires have materialized since first writing them down, but it also gives insights into your mental framework and the influences in your life at the time of writing. If you should have a lot of items to add to the list, you may just want to redo the spell.

However, you may not want to keep the list around, or, for symbolic reasons, you may want to consign your wishes to the elements as an additional affirmation that they're in the care of the powers of the Universe. There are a number of ways to dispose of your list: you can burn your list in the fireplace and then scatter the ashes to the wind or water, you can bury it in your backyard near the root of a tree or under a religious statue, or place it in the crotch of a tree (as long as it's in you own yard so you're not littering). You can make a ceremony out of disposing of your list by saying:

*I give my wishes to the keeping
   of the Higher Powers.
Borne by the elements,
In the care of the Universe.
So it is, and so it shall be!*

When the envelope has been put away or disposed of, waste no time in heading out for the fun outing you have planned.

Priming the Pump

It is possible to "prime the pump," to get magic flowing in the direction of your goals (whether for your back burner list or your secondary list), and it's not really cheating. You can create situations where you can't help but get what you want, even if you use ordinary physical means and no magic is seemingly involved. Priming the pump has magical validity. It could be described as a form of imitative magic, where you go through actions that symbolize the outcomes you want. Setting yourself up for success also serves as a positive affirmation, a symbolic act that opens channels of energy to bring things your way. It reinforces the belief in your unconscious mind and in your personal universe that you have abundance, that good things are coming to you.

To get a jump start on making things happen for you, take out your secondary goals list, and put a check mark alongside items that are relatively inexpensive and not difficult to obtain through ordinary means. Designate an arbitrary amount of time for the thing to manifest: say a fortnight, a month, or a Moon cycle. If there's a magical suggestion or spell in this book that's appropriate for manifesting the thing you want, you can perform that, or just use creative visualization techniques, affirmations, or other appropriate techniques that you can find in other books on magic and positive thinking. If the thing doesn't magically fall into your lap before this period is over, simply go out and buy yourself one or obtain one through any other honest means available to you. (You can bring in a few items this way if you choose to do the Good Things Coming In spell in Chapter 8, which requires that you bring something special into your home each day, even if it's only a small token or symbolic thing.)

Another way to prime the pump is to let your friends and relatives know that you're looking for certain things on your check list—the things that have been noted as simple, inexpensive, and not too hard to obtain. That way, if they happen to come across any of these things at a bargain or a garage sale, or just have some of these items sitting around in the attic, or hear of someone who wants to get rid of same, they'll think of you. Most of us are, after all, always on the lookout for nice things for our friends and relatives. However, the main problem often is that we don't have a clear idea of what they want, or it may seem like they already have everything. What's more, if you have friends and relatives with whom you feel comfortable enough to confide that you're embarking on this playful magic, and that you're going after these goals, they might think it's fun to play along with you and help you out.

Setting aside special days for yourself is another way to set yourself up for magical gifts. It's important that you declare your intention out loud, saying, "This is MY day." This is based on the ancient magical notion that when you say a thing is true, it is true, at least as a template on the Ethereal Plane. By declaring "This is MY day," you make an imprint on the Unconscious Mind/Ethereal

Planes that opens channels for your type of things to come to you. You can also prime the pump by scheduling some type of activity, outing, or celebration to reinforce the idea that it's YOUR day. You can go to certain expenses, like buying a cake or going out to dinner or a movie. However, if you enjoy simple things like outings in the park or going camping, you can minimize expenses. You can declare special days once a week or once a month, depending on what your schedule will allow. Naturally, you'll also want to set aside days for your other family members, where they get to choose what to do or where to go, and which you can reinforce by doing favors and giving them extra consideration on those days.

I originally realized that this was a magical technique when on school vacations, I arranged special days for each of my kids. We would go to places of their own choosing, usually related to their distinct personal interests, and everything went well. However, we also noticed that a lot of serendipitous things were happening on those days, and they were always in line with the special interests of whoever's day it was. This was like the icing on the cake.

When Magic Doesn't Work

Although I'm such a believer in the art of magic working, I have to admit that there are some magical goals that I and others I know have not yet been able to achieve. The fact is, despite how much energy and focus you direct into positive thinking, affirmations, visualizations, rituals, and spells, sometimes the best magical efforts come to nothing.

I often use a working definition of magic as "nudging possibilities and probabilities." With this in mind, one can see that sometimes there are too many negatives, too many outside factors and variables, or too many other forces aligned against a magical objective, thereby greatly reducing the probabilities involved. As discussed in Chapter 1, desperation and negative emotions can also work against magic by acting as negative affirmations. And of course, if we accept the idea that there are some greater destinies that we may not always be aware of, then it's possible that some things are just not meant to be.

However, I've found that the number one obstacle to magical success is cross purposes, that is, when you have two conflicting issues. This is most likely to occur when the different facets of your personality have motivations that do not run parallel to each other. It's perhaps easiest to work magic to attract minor things, rather than major things, because there are fewer potential objections to your having them.

Most of my magical successes and serendipitous windfalls have occurred in attracting small things to me. For example, while on a vacation, I bought my kids some small fluorite and pyrite crystals at a rock shop. Unfortunately, the fluorite got broken and the pyrite was stolen. So, I made a mental note to myself that when the opportunity came up, I'd just get them some bigger, better samples. Not long thereafter, I was out walking and came upon a garage sale offering 15 cents each for some beautiful and sizeable fluorite and pyrite specimens that would have cost $7.00 each at a rock shop or New Age store, plus an extra bonus, amethyst geodes at 50 cents each, which would have cost around $14.00 ordinarily. I hadn't done any conscious magic to obtain these items. I hadn't even given the matter any further thought. However, in noting that they were desirable, I believe that my Unconscious went to work on it. What's more, there was no reason why we shouldn't have them. Since they sit on a windowsill, they don't take up much space, and there is no other objection or any conflicting needs that would be at odds with our having these crystals.

On the other hand, here is an example of a larger issue where there are a lot of cross purposes involved. I would like to live in the deep wilderness, but at the same time I want to be able to live in a place where there are good social, educational, and job opportunities for myself and my children. There are other conflicting factors as well, both for myself and other family members. I'm still working on sorting things out, evaluating what I really want, learning to be resourceful enough to have some things both ways, and making progress breaking these things down into smaller issues which can be dealt with individually.

So you see, it's the larger issues that tend to bring us into cross purposes. That's why the philosophy of playful magic favors directing your magical efforts toward having fun and achieving the minor things on your goals list, while submitting the larger issues to the Higher Powers through the Back Burner spell or other methods such as prayer and faith. In looking over the major issues on your goals list, consider what conflicting purposes may be giving you resistance. Sometimes you can break the larger issues down into smaller components that you can sort out. Also, directing attention to the smaller things can allow time and freedom for changes in consciousness and circumstances to take place, creating a smoother path for attaining your deeper desires.

Frivolous Things in the Service of Individuation

I would like to point out one more advantage of working toward goals on your secondary list. The types of qualities, hobbies, skills, and diversions that emerge as you develop your secondary list items may, in the long run, come to have more personal meaning and impact on your life than the security issues which now seem so important. Because those items are chosen for fun, not out of the duress imposed by the drive for security (or the drives of the id or the ego), they're more likely to satisfy our personal "individuation" or "core creativity." (When the sense of security is at stake, we're more susceptible to the dictates of society or opinions of others, that is, traditionally accepted views on what you need to do to get ahead in this world.) By allowing yourself to kill time, engage in frivolous things, and be open to

playful opportunities, the deeper needs of the Self are able to emerge and find expression, and that really opens the floodgates for magical synchronicity. In *Synchronicity—Science, Myth, and the Trickster,* Allan Combs and Mark Holland have synthesized a lot of different philosophers' views that are in agreement on this matter, including those of Joseph Campbell, Bill Moyers, Ira Progroff, and Carl Jung, stating:

> ...when you choose to follow your bliss, when you make choices based upon an inner sense of fulfillment rather than outer demands, there is often a sense of 'hidden hands,' of unexpected opportunities and unanticipated resources. This is synchronicity in the service of individuation. It is the influence of the Self in the world of human affairs that makes itself felt when we submit to the deep call of our being. Carl Jung termed this the law of synchronicity, meaning that when we are in accord with an archetypal process, then that archetype, in this case the Self, can influence events around us even at a distance, as in the old Taoist saying, "The right man sitting in his house and thinking the right thought will be heard a hundred miles distant."[4]

So the secondary goals are more likely to be ones that you intuitively realize will enable your to follow your bliss and find that path with heart and meaning.

Showing Gratitude for the Good Stuff

Always remember to give thanks for fulfilled wishes and other bits of good luck that come your way. Acknowledging these things serves as a positive affirmation, and the things that we affirm increase. Thankfulness also gives energy back to the Universe. To acknowledge and reinforce your luck, you can do some of the following things whenever something good comes to you, or whenever you receive some other kind of blessing:

- Light a thank-you candle and burn it for ten minutes to half an hour. Keep a very large white candle on hand just for this purpose. Carve an "X" on the candle. This is the rune Gebo, and in this context represents a joyful synergy, the exchange of energies between the Self and the Universe. (See Appendix I, if you would like to know how to do extra magical preparation of candles.)

- Drop a penny or a pebble in a big glass jar, so that you can see how your good fortune is building up. If you use pennies, plan to buy some small treat or trinket when you've collected enough, or donate them to your favorite cause.

- Have a calendar with very large squares for the days. Put a special sticker, such as a gold star or red heart, on the calendar to mark every fortuitous happening.

- Have a little celebration or buy small souvenirs for yourself—something you may collect, such as polished stones or small crystals.

- Give an offering to Mother Nature or her creatures by sprinkling some cornmeal on the ground (a Native

American custom with ancient Slavic and Teutonic parallels), or scatter some other grain or bird seed.

- Make use of one of those big posters or New Age coloring books that features intricate designs with lots of small segments that you color in yourself, usually with felt tip pens in bright, jewel-like colors. There are even mandalas available in this form. Color in a new segment each time you count a new blessing.

- Add a bead to a cord, which can be turned into a necklace or garland once you've strung enough beads.

Endnotes

1. For further information on the use of positive affirmations, see Appendix IV.

2. Renee, Janina. *Tarot Spells.* St. Paul: Llewellyn, 1990.

3. Be aware that turning your cares over to the Higher Powers doesn't mean you get out of your duties. Taking care of the needs of the minute includes showing up at work on time, fulfilling your responsibilities to your children, and so on.

4. Combs, Allan, and Holland, Mark. *Synchronicity—Science, Myth, and the Trickster.* New York: Paragon House, 1990.

Chapter 4

Your Playful Personality

Each individual contains within himself or herself the entire spectrum of human traits. Of course, no two of us are alike because each one possesses different characteristics to different degrees. We all have certain personal traits that we express more frequently and more easily, while there are other characteristics that we do not readily express, though we may admire them in others.

Individual personalities can be blessed with some very different and unique qualities of imagination, humor, creativity, curiosity, spontaneity, and adventurousness. When the playful impulses that are in harmony with our own personality types are given free expression, they allow us to feel joyous and "in sync" with ourselves and the world. They bring that sense of deep personal satisfaction that comes with actualizing the Self.

However, some of the playful activities which we, as certain personality types, would not normally engage in, can also be valuable and meaningful to us. By exploring modes of play that we would not normally go out for, we can open the doors to some very profound experiences. It is in so doing that we push our boundaries. It enables us to open channels that wouldn't be available to us if we just stuck to the things with which we feel most comfortable. We are privileged with new insights, new sources of creativity, and even a potential for mystical experience. The Jungians have especially found this to be true in their studies of the conscious functions of personality, pointing out that an individual's less preferred functions are closer to the realm of the Unconscious, and therefore bound up with mystical and symbolic meanings, as well as synchronistic experiences.

Thus, by having a good sense of who you are, you can find satisfaction by making time and indulging yourself in some of the things you find naturally enjoyable. You don't have to feel guilty about the seeming waste of time when you realize that these things will energize and renew you. You can also encourage spontaneity, satisfy curiosity, and find material, as well as psychic, rewards by occasionally experimenting with modes of recreation that are less familiar or ones in which you feel less proficient. (Although you may have to approach the latter a little more slowly and cautiously.)

There have been numerous studies of personality—philosophies that shed light on all imaginable personality types and all the facets of personality in all of its infinite variations. These theories are useful toward understanding where our unique personal strengths are, as well as what areas appear to us as undiscovered territory—places that can evoke our fears, as well as lay open great riches for us. Studies of personality can range from ancient and traditional systems such as astrology, palmistry, and the Tarot, to modern approaches such as Freudian, Jungian, theories pertaining to birth order, body types, blood types, and so on. No personality theory can provide a truly complete picture of any person, but all of these systems are ways to shed light on at least some facets of different individual's characters.

Understanding personality can naturally be helpful to the practice of playful magic by showing us our individual paths to fulfillment, as well as those desperation areas that we're looking for creative and carefree ways to work around. Naturally, it would be impossible to touch on all of those different theories here. However, I will provide two different approaches, looking at an ancient belief that four elements express themselves in human character, as well as a theory of the different functions of personality as outlined by Jung and developed by Briggs-Myers.

Elemental Types

In ancient times, it was common for philosophers, scientists, and alchemists to believe that the physical world, as well as a corresponding spiritual world, was comprised of four elements: Fire, Earth, Air, and Water. (Some added an intangible fifth element, Spirit, to bind them all together.) This belief was found not only in the Western world, but in many other parts of the world as well. The model of the four elements is no longer of use to modern scientists, but it is still a meaningful philosophical system, and is used in astrology and the Tarot, as well as in numerous magical and mystical philosophies and practices.

The philosophy of the four elements has been applied to many different things, including ways in which these elements can manifest in people. Ideally, a person would have a balance of the four elements. However, certain individuals may have especially strong affinities to a single element. In fact, some health and personality problems are seen as being linked to an overabundance of one element in an individual's constitution.

Individuals' affinities to the elements are often pointed out by astrologers, with the signs relating to the Fire element are Aries, Leo, and Sagittarius; the Earth signs are Taurus, Virgo, and Capricorn; the Air signs are Gemini, Libra, and Aquarius; and the Water signs are Cancer, Scorpio, and Pisces. Whether you have strong affinities with a certain element is determined not merely by your sun sign, but also the other planets' positions in your chart. Needless to say, if a lot of your planets are stacked in certain signs or houses, you may exhibit an overemphasis on one element, while persons with planets more evenly distributed would be considered to be more balanced. Also, different planetary transits can cause certain elemental influences to be more heavily felt at certain times.

Some psychics and magical philosophers believe there are spiritual beings called elementals, who are manifestations or expressions of the element's spiritual being. Air elementals are called sylphs, Fire elementals salamanders, Earth elementals gnomes, and Water elementals are undines. (The novel, *Undine,* by de la Motte Foque, is about an elemental who wants to become human.)

Some psychically sensitive persons are of the opinion that elementals are just a mindless, soulless, and temporary sort of phenomena, created in those moments when the minds of people touch the mind of nature. However, there are other psychics who claim that elementals have lives, minds, and existence in their own right, independent of any contact with humans. Furthermore, those who believe that elementals can be strong individual entities feel that they can sometimes incarnate as human beings. Indeed, they suggest that some humans may have first gotten their start that way. The ones that are new to the cycle of human incarnation would exhibit the pure characteristics of their element. They are said to be very charming and that by being around them you can very strongly experience the energies of their element, though it is also observed that they can be unbalanced in some areas of human experience. Elemental humans who have an opportunity to live through more human incarnations can gradually become more rounded, however.[1] Along with astrological factors, the belief in the potential of humans to have had elemental incarnations has contributed to the idea of elemental personality types.

Whether or not you believe in elemental spirits or are familiar with your personal horoscope, you can see that most of us have some elemental characteristics. You can judge whether you or the people you know have special elemental affinities by observing behavior, modes of expression, and likes and dislikes.

In spotting an elemental type, an obvious giveaway is what sort of environment the person is attracted to. Air people like high places and big sky country, though they are also fascinated by cities with their tall buildings, skylines, and active intellectual and social life. Earth people appreciate agricultural areas and wilderness areas where they can blend into the natural environment. They also feel secure in small towns where laborers, tradespeople, and people who work with their hands are more valued. Fire people like to be in cities and other places where the action is, but they also have an affinity for deserts and places that other people might consider waste areas. Water people find coastlines, river towns, places with lush greenery, and resort areas to be very compelling.

Following are brief descriptions of elemental personality types, focusing on their playful qualities, as well as ways to use each element's energies to create balance, or to get more of the influence of a particular element. (You can treat some minor physical and psychological complaints this way, but naturally, you should always seek proper medical help for more major or persistent problems.)[2]

Fire

Strong Fire personalities bring high energy and exuberance to everything they do, including their favorite forms of recreation. They like to do active, physical, and adventurous things. They are lively and creative, and their friends can be ignited by the Fire person's enthusiasm, although they may find it difficult to keep up with him or her. When at play, they are spontaneous and willing to take risks, and can enjoy themselves purely, without worrying about what other people think. Their positive characteristics are initiative, passion, and warmth. On the negative side, the caricature of a Fire personality can be volatile, violent, insufferably egotistical, and lacking emotional empathy and understanding of others.

An excess of Fire energies can make a person too impulsive, too pushy, and insensitive. Excess Fire can also produce insomnia, a feeling of being "wired," and other types of nervousness.

Bringing in the influences of other elements might moderate excess Fire, enabling that person to make sounder decisions and maintain self-control. A good way to do this is by grounding that energy in meaningful Earth activities, such as caring for the physical needs of others: baking wholesome food, giving back rubs, and just lending a helping hand. Another way is to use up that energy through strenuous physical activities. The aerobic nature of certain sports employs the Air element as a way of channeling the Fire element. Getting out into nature, especially where the kingdoms of Earth, Air, and Water converge, is very balancing. Another way to tone down the excess Fire is to cut back on caffeine and excess social activities, if these are a problem for you.

If you are experiencing fatigue, low metabolism, poor circulation, feeling cold, or having coldness in your extremities, do visualizations where you picture yourself being bathed in elemental Fire and generating fire from within. Then, get moving. Go out and do something physically active. If you have been unusually sedentary, you may have to do this in small steps, such as taking a short, 20-minute walk, and gradually escalating your levels of activity. In Chapter 12, the suggestions for playful ways to attune to the Moon's transit through Aries, Leo, and Sagittarius can also give you ideas on how to experience the energies of the Fire element.

Earth

A person with a strong affinity for the Earth element may be quiet and subtle, or boisterous, and, well, "earthy." The more refined Earth types like to create beautiful settings and beautiful experiences for their friends and family. The not-quite-so-refined types at least are able to make you feel at home, you can relax and put your feet up when visiting them, there's no need to put on airs. People with positive Earth qualities are also appreciated for their calm strength and supportiveness. Their understanding of life's physical conditions and demands enables them to be good nurturers, not only of people, but of plants and animals. They can be very conscientious, productive people who are good at mastering skills, focusing on detail work, and carrying things through. Negative Earth types can be crude, clumsy, and callous, as well as blindly materialistic, selfish, and miserly. They can act as dampers on the emotions of others, and weigh down the progress of others with their negativity and resistance to change.

If you feel like you're digging yourself into a rut, or your friends are accusing you of being a "stick in the mud," you're probably laden with an overabundance of Earth influences. On days when you're apathetic and slow to act, or feel sluggish and clumsier than usual, this is also apt to be the case. Over emphasis of elemental Earth can also make you so preoccupied with security that you have a mounting sense of fear and find it hard to break away from work and allow time for recreation.

If you want to overcome the more oppressive influences of this element, involve yourself in fun, carefree, active things. Do things with friends that will help keep you moving along, like joining a group hike, or dance, sparring, and physical exercise routines that require a buddy. Seek out events where you can get swept up in positive crowd activities, such as peaceful rallies, concerts, and fairs. You can also generate greater personal creative fertility by bringing in some of the sensitivity and fine tuning of the Water element by devoting time to emotional and spiritual concerns.

If you recognize a need to ground yourself, concentrate on Earth element activities. Learn a new skill and apply yourself to crafts and other projects that let you work with your hands.

Rhythmical crafts like crochet and knitting can be especially calming. Also, explore types of play that give pleasure to the senses. If you lack a sense of material security, mitigate this somewhat by calling upon your inner resourcefulness to give you ideas for ways in which you can improve the beauty and comfort of your surroundings, whatever they may be. Also, you can consult Chapter 12, and consider the suggestions for playful ways to attune to the Moon's transit through Taurus, Virgo, and Capricorn to get ideas on living the energies of the Earth element.

Air

People who possess the positive qualities of the Air element have a noticeable sense of levity, buoyancy, and lightness. This element is associated with mentality, bestowing clarity of thought and expansiveness of mind, a lively sense of curiosity, creativity, inventiveness, the ability to play with words, and an appreciation and knack for jokes, puns, riddles. This is the element most identified with humor. Air people like games of all kinds, and are able to make games out of life's routines, business, and interactions. They also find fun in learning. The Air personalty is adventurous, spontaneous, and quick to appreciate new things. On the dark side, a person who has developed the most negative characteristics of the Air element tends to be haughty, coldly calculating, detached, cynical, sarcastic, and mentally and verbally abusive.

You experience an excess of elemental Air influences at those times when you can't focus your thoughts, are spacey or distracted, are hyper, or have your head in the clouds. This can also show itself in nervousness and free-floating anxiety. Insomnia can result from too much Air and Fire energy building in the head and not being dispersed outward. Spending too much time thinking about things, and not getting around to actually doing them, can also be a problem of the Air personality.

To correct an imbalance of this element, consider enjoyable but relaxing ways to ground yourself. Engage in the quiet pleasures of

the Earth element, including handcrafts, gardening, sensual comforts like massage, and just spending time close to nature. To mitigate negative Air characteristics, open yourself to the empathic, feeling qualities of the Water element, showing compassion and loyalty, and sharing good times with friends and family.

To get more of the positive qualities of the Air element, immerse yourself in different forms of humor—exchanging jokes, watching comedy shows, sending humorous greeting cards, and so on. Committing yourself to physical regimens that emphasize gracefulness and precision of movement, such as dance and the martial arts, attunes you to the lightness of the Air element, while at the same time providing the discipline to ground and focus it. Also, devote time to cultural activities that stimulate the intellect, as well as the senses, such as listening to music, visiting art galleries, and reading and writing poetry. In Chapter 12, the suggestions for playful ways to attune to the Moon's transit through Gemini, Libra, and Aquarius can also give you ideas on how to celebrate the energies of the Air element.

Water

A person who identifies with the positive qualities of the Water element can be friendly, romantic, responsive, sensitive, empathic, compassionate, giving, emotionally open to others, and ready to share the good times. They can be loyal friends, good listeners, and offer a sympathetic shoulder to cry on. They love their homes, children, and animals. Water people are creative, intuitive, idealistic, and able to translate the stuff of dreams into beautiful forms. They have the desire to look deep within and the ability to draw their friends into their own mystical realm.

On the other hand, persons with very negative Water characteristics can be emotional tyrants, manipulating and layering on guilt, and being emotionally dependent to the point of being psychic vampires. They can be too preoccupied with their own problems, masochistic, and passive to the point of not being able to do anything for themselves. This Water type is in real danger of addiction and dissipation.

If you are prone to, or are experiencing, depression and moodiness, you may be awash in the emotional tides that come with an excess of Water elemental influences. When a person is being influenced by excess Water he or she may be overly sensitive, weak or soft, and full of good intentions that never come to anything. If you feel that other people have too much power over you, that you are being pulled in too many directions, you have a hard time saying no, and are experiencing difficulty making decisions and taking action, this is also likely to be the case.

If you are concerned about being too wishy-washy, do something that's playful, but bold and determined—something that combines the Fire quality of courage and the Earth quality of stick-to-it-iveness. Find other ways to develop the "take charge" qualities of the Fire signs. Get out and go places. Look at interesting things and people to distract you from your own too deeply felt concerns.

If you've been living in a situation of emotional deprivation that has left you feeling physically withered and dried-out emotionally, you can invoke some of the moist nourishing powers of elemental Water by trying to get in touch with your intuitive and unconscious nature through dream analysis, meditative and spiritual practices, divination, artistic expression, keeping a personal journal, and other forms of therapy and self-help that encourage knowledge of the Deep Self. Also, spend time by water sources such as seas, lakes, and rivers. You can also consult Chapter 12; its suggestions for playful ways to be in harmony with the Moon's transit through Cancer, Scorpio, and Pisces, can give you additional ideas on how to celebrate the qualities of the Water element.

It could be said that the ancient belief in four elemental types gives us a feeling for the energies of Nature. To look at another way an understanding personality can open wellsprings of energy and new channels of opportunity, we move on to a modern theory relating to the functions of human consciousness.

The Functions of the Conscious Personality

The personality types to be described in this section were delineated in the 1950s by Isabel Briggs-Myers and her mother, Katharine Briggs, as an expansion of some of Carl Jung's theories.[3] This system looks at human personalities in terms of four pairs of functions, which can be seen as areas of human life, choices for interpreting and acting on one's own inner and outer worlds.[4] These modes of experiencing life and reality are the opposing duos of extroversion-introversion (E-I), sensing-intuition (S-N), thinking-feeling (T-F), and judging-perceiving (J-P). It's the combination of these four choices that makes the psychological type. These types are coded with the use of the initials, so there are 16 different combinations. For example, an introverted, intuitive, feeling, perceiving person would be an INFP, (note that intuition uses the letter "N" because "I" is already taken). This system creates personality profiles that are informative, detailed, and give lots of specifics.

People who are new to this concept are confused by this alphabet soup, so I'll treat it in a very simplified manner. Also, due to limitations in the scope of this book, I can't go into these functions in much depth or detail, for which I apologize. The following is a quick and concise overview of these polarities.

Extroversion-Introversion

Extroversion-Introversion (E-I) describes whether you draw your energy from inner or outer sources. Extroverts are oriented to and draw their energy from the outer world, especially from contact with other people. Introverts draw their energy from their inner life. They also have different comfort zones: Introverts are more territorial and like more "personal space," one of the reasons they tend to be homebodies. Extroverts can feel comfortable almost anywhere, enjoy more physical closeness, and have a greater sense of connectedness with people.

Sensing-Intuition

Sensing-Intuition (S-N) refers to how you gather and process information. These are different ways of thinking about things, of experiencing the world, of approaching reality—something that is often a great source of miscommunication between people. Sensation types have a strong awareness of what is happening here and now in the "real world," and are very good at noticing details. Intuitives are tuned in to inner voices, so to speak, and can fail to observe things that are happening right under their noses. Their awareness is unfocused, picking up on a variety of conflicting subliminal stimuli simultaneously. However, Ns can get insights that bring a lot of disparate elements together in new and creative ways. Because they can visualize possibilities, Ns are very concerned with the future, whereas S types, who are more interested in objective facts, are oriented to the concerns of the moment.

Thinking-Feeling

Thinking-Feeling (T-F) refers to the way we make decisions, not the actual quality or intensity of our feelings or intellect. (So don't mistake this to mean that every thinker is an Einstein or that every feeler is a Mother Theresa.) Thinkers tend to make decisions by evaluating information through logical and impersonal processes, and feelers prefer to make decisions based on personal, emotional impact. This doesn't mean that Ts don't have deep feelings, or that Fs are unintelligent; it's just a different way of handling choices. There are a number of sources of misunderstanding between Ts and Fs, one being that their emotional responses can be out of sync with each other.

Judging-Perceiving

Judging-Perceiving (J-P) is the function that relates to how you structure your time and the other elements in your life. Judgers like to have things planned and organized; closure is very important to them. Perceivers are more flexible, open to more influences, open to outcome. Another observable difference is that Js are oriented to product, while Ps are oriented to process. Significant to our subject matter, Ps are seen as being more playful and having more fun. Js have difficulty relaxing and having fun until they've cleared all of their work out of the way, while Ps can take time to stop and smell the roses without feeling guilty or pressured.

It's important to emphasize that these functions pertain to preferences. Each person may use all of these counterpart functions to varying degrees, but habitually prefers to rely on some more than others. Thus, a person who is a sensing type may use his or her intuitive faculties from time to time, but prefers to get information from concrete, objective sources. A person who is an extrovert may find it rewarding to spend time alone, but more often seeks the company of other people, while an introvert may enjoy socializing but then needs to go home to recharge. When one has a less preferred function, there's a tendency to try to get someone else to take care of it; a thinking person might have a feeling spouse who spends more time listening to and sympathizing with the emotional woes of both partner's relatives.

Jungians tend to take the position that everyone has one most preferred or "superior" function, and it's opposite is his or her least preferred, or "inferior" function. The superior function is what you feel you can do best, so you spend more time developing it. Its counterpart, the inferior function, is the one you feel least comfortable with, so you try to avoid it or fob it off on other people. The rest of the functions, then, are the auxiliary functions. (Although the less preferred auxiliary functions are inferior functions in comparison to their preferred counterparts.)

The auxiliary functions can offer a lot of opportunities for playfulness. As von Franz points out:

> Switching over to an auxiliary function takes place when one feels that the present way of living has become lifeless, when one gets more or less constantly bored with oneself and one's activities...The best way to know how to switch is simply to say: 'All right...Where in my past life is an activity that I feel I could still enjoy? An activity out of which I could still get a kick? If a person then genuinely picks up that activity, he will see that he has switched over to another function.[5]

One of the most significant insights to come out of this study of functions (and which affects magical thinking), is the recognition that accessing the inferior function can lead to intensely meaningful experiences—even those magical and psychical experiences that we ascribe to synchronicity. This is because the inferior function remains bound to the Unconscious. At a certain point in life, a lot of people start to get in touch with the inferior function as they come more in contact with the realm of the Unconscious. With this comes the discovery of new sources of energy, and even psychic revelations. Von Franz recognizes this phenomenon, explaining:

> In the realm of the inferior function there is a great concentration of life, so that as soon as the superior function is worn out—begins to rattle and lose oil like an old car—if people succeed in turning to their inferior function they will rediscover a new potential of life. Everything in the realm of the inferior function becomes exciting, dramatic, full of positive and negative possibilities.[6]

Thus, getting in touch with the auxiliary and inferior functions creates a greater sense of wholeness.

Using Your Functions Playfully

Like the study of elemental affinities, the theory of functions can apply to doing the things you enjoy, as well as the playful magic approach, which encourages curiosity, creativity, spontaneity, and stepping outside of boundaries.

The recreational things you have a natural preference for will be more relaxing and fulfilling for you, so those should be the type of activities to retreat into when you're under stress. However, when you're ready for change and challenge, when you want to stir that magical cauldron of circumstance, it's a good time to experiment with modes of play that you normally wouldn't consider. Going against the inclinations of your type is a way to push your magical boundaries, and indeed, sometimes an unconscious recognition of a need for change will create such inner prompting. It is through the light-hearted things that we can touch on our auxiliary and inferior functions in ways that are less stressful or force us to step too far out of our comfort zones.

When you try to do something that requires you to use the functions you're less comfortable with, it can be pretty frustrating. However, this is also more challenging, so there's a greater potential of reward and accomplishment on those occasions when you are able to perform such a function in a capable manner. Some of the most meaningful "peak experiences"—times when you really feel you're hitting your stride—involve the recognition that you're doing well in a function that is normally intimidating for you. These are uniquely magical experiences when you get the feeling that something in Earth or Heaven (or at least in the Unconscious), has moved for you.

One way that you can approach your more inferior functions in a playful manner is to engage in activities where the weaker functions are necessary but are bolstered by the stronger capabilities. For example, an activity that engages my stronger functions but also enables me to deal with my weaker functions in a pleasant and satisfying way is bird watching, or "birding." I realize that, although this is a playful pursuit for me, it's the sort of thing that might make a lot of other people die of boredom. However, it's just a matter of course that different people are going to find challenge, renewal, and excitement in different things.

To give you an idea of how this works for me, I'll tell you a little bit about myself: I'm an INTJ, (Introverted-Intuitive-Thinking-Judgmental person), which means that I'm out of my element when I must go out into the world and deal with people (extroversion), utilize observation skills (sensing), tune in to the emotions of those around me (feeling), and be flexible and open to outcome (perceiving).

Birding is usually a solitary activity for me, but it does encourage me to get out and around. Because my powers of observation are pretty woeful, I consider it a major accomplishment that I've learned to distinguish between certain look-alike species. At the same time, I use intuitive qualities, speculating on what they do and where they go, and what is to become of them with all of this massive environmental despoliation. This hobby has affected my deeper levels of intuition too: bird imagery dominates my dreaming. Identifying and gathering information on bird species also engages the thinking and judging functions. I bring in the feeling and perceiving functions (in an intuitive way) by taking an interest in the personal lives and individual personalities of my feathered neighbors, trying to perceive and feel their energies (They are truly beings of energy, and you can learn a lot about energy patterns by watching them.), and reaching out to them with love, as well as by just appreciating the fact that they're there—they exist.

Another way to get to know your less preferred functions is to make small, cautious forays into those areas, preferably in situations where there's minimal stress but worthwhile rewards, or give yourself little rewards for your accomplishments in these areas.

In concluding this chapter, I want to mention that an added

benefit of getting in touch with your inferior functions is that they offer greater intensity of experience, due to their connection to the Unconscious realm. Thus, an extroverted sensing person who takes up meditation and goes within is likely to have more profound and moving insights than the introverted intuitive types who go inside their heads all the time. Conversely, when an intuitive person, who isn't normally too aware of his or her physical surroundings, does switch focus to the outer world, the observations are more vivid—sounds, smells, colors, etc., all seem more intense and pregnant with meaning.

Endnotes

1. Back in the seventies, there seemed to be a lot of discussion of elementals and elemental type people. One doesn't hear these ideas expressed as often nowadays. There's still room for a lot of speculation as to whether elementals can have human incarnations.

2. Marcia Starck's book, *Earth Mother Astrology,* offers lots of techniques for balancing elemental excesses, as well as other astrological influences (St. Paul: Llewellyn, 1989).

3. Information on the Jungian and Myers-Briggs types drawn from the following sources: Keirsey, David, and Bates, Marilyn, *Please Understand Me: Character and Temperament Types* (Del Mar: Prometheus Nemesis Book Company, 1984); von Franz, Marie-Louise *Lectures on Jung's Typology: The Inferior Function* (Dallas: Spring Publications, 1971); Hillman, James, *The Feeling Function;* and Jeffries, William C., *True To Type* (Norfolk: Hampton Roads Publishing, 1991).

4. Note: although we have sets of fours here, they don't perfectly correspond to the elemental types, though there are certain similarities. Different writers have linked the Jungian types to the elemental types for philosophical purposes, but have some disagreement as to which goes with which. Thus, some would link Water to sensing and Earth to feeling, while others would do the opposite. There's something about the number four that allows itself to serve as the structure for

a lot of religious, philosophical, and psychological models.

5. von Franz, Marie-Louise. *Lectures on Jung's Typology: The Inferior Function.* Dallas: Spring Publications, 1971. Page 73.

6. Ibid. Page 15.

Chapter 5

Chakra Stimulation Exercise

This chapter outlines a simple exercise you can perform when you want a tonic that will both relax and refresh you, and focus your mind and body on the playful qualities of spontaneity, joyousness, aliveness, and creativity.

This exercise is designed to gently stimulate your body's energy centers, known as the chakras. The chakras are the body's main energy centers, as perceived by many psychics and defined in various Eastern metaphysical traditions. These energy centers are aligned according to the colors in the spectrum, and they tend to correspond to a number of major organs.

Because there's something very practical, fundamental, and appealing about using the chakra system, various chakra stimulation exercises are being incorporated into a wide variety of psychic awareness and healing disciplines.[1] A lot of ordinary people are finding ways to use knowledge of the chakras to enhance their physical and emotional health. Entertainer and author Shirley

MacLaine has been especially effective in making an understanding of the chakra system accessible to large numbers of people.[2]

This exercise combines mental focus on the chakra; visualization of its color energy; some physical stimulation of that area through muscle contraction, effleurage, or other means; and the saying of affirmations. In addition to enabling you to become more aware of your energy centers, this exercise will help you feel more balanced and vital, open to experience, and will put you in greater attunement with your body, with other people, with the forces of Nature, and with what's happening in the world around you.[3]

Note that when the instructions say words like feel, visualize, or envision, as in "feel the sensation…" or "visualize the energy being drawn…", the exercise calls for combining your own physical sensing with mental visualization. Those who are new at doing this kind of imaging may have to rely solely on imagination (i.e., fantasy), but you'll find that, with practice, the actual physical sensations become very perceptible.

To prepare for this exercise, sit or lie in a comfortable position. (If you can, perform this outdoors where you can touch the Earth.) Relax and breathe deeply and rhythmically for about five minutes, clearing your mind as you do so. Focus your attention on your feet. You can wiggle your toes, flex your feet a little, and press them against the ground to become more aware of sensation. Feel warmth and power being drawn up through your feet, through your legs, and into the trunk of your body—drawn from the solid Earth herself. Concentrate on this sensation for a few minutes, or for whatever length of time you feel comfortable.

Focus your mind on your first chakra, known as the root chakra or *Muladhara,* which is situated at the base of your spine, the area of your coccyx. *Muladhara's* qualities are security and the pleasure derived from stability, strength, survival, and the feeling of being grounded.

Through this center, which is the foundation of your chakra system, you are energized by the nourishing Earth Spirit.

You may visualize the vortex of energy being stimulated and generated in this area as a radiant red flower opening its petals. Contract the muscles in this area, then gently relax them. Envision that the energy, which continues to be drawn up through your feet, comes from the great womb and the burning heart's core of the Earth, up through the ground, up into your root chakra. Feel the warmth generated in this area circulating throughout your body to make you feel warm and alive. After you have concentrated on these sensations and images for several minutes, or whatever interval of time is comfortable, say aloud:

I draw energy from the Earth,
my source and my provider.
I draw deep from her fiery core.
Her ancient blood flows through me,
energizing my being.
I celebrate the strength
that is rooted within me
as I draw energy upward into my being.
I celebrate the gifts and resources
that the Earth provides me.

Next, direct your attention upward. Feel the drawn energy spreading upward in a spectrum, transiting from red to orange, to the second chakra, in the general area below your navel. This is known as the sacral chakra or *Svadhisthana,* which is variously translated as "sweetness," or "that which belongs to itself." It encompasses the sexual organs, spleen, and kidneys.

Through this center, you are connected with the body of your emotions, and the animal energies. Much of our vitality, creativity, and enthusiasm derives from the primal energy of this center.

This chakra enables us to experience our bond with all of the animal world, as well as our physical attraction to others through body chemistry. Its qualities are pride, enthusiasm, excitement, passion, pleasure, sexuality, fertility, and being present and taking pleasure in one's own body.

Visualize the vortex of energy being stimulated and generated in this area as a rich orange flower opening its petals. Contract the muscles in this area, then gently relax them. Envision that the column of energy is drawn up into this second chakra. Feel the heat generated in this area filling you with a joyful aliveness. After you have concentrated on these sensations and images for several minutes, or whatever interval of time is comfortable, say aloud:

> *I am filled with wild enthusiasm,*
> > *swept up in the enjoyment of life.*
> *I am free to be myself,*
> > *without holding back.*
> *I can be wild and crazy,*
> > *bold and adventurous.*
> *I'm willing to be silly and risk embarrassment,*
> > *in sharing fun times with my friends.*
> *I take pleasure in the dance of life.*
> *I celebrate the uniqueness of me.*

Now, move your focus upward. Feel the column of energy extending upward in a spectrum, transiting from orange to gold to bright yellow, to the solar plexus chakra, a broad area that extends from around your navel to the hollow area between your ribs. It is known as *Manipura,* which is variously translated as "City of Jewels," or "Lustrous Gem." The physical parts associated with this chakra include the stomach, liver, large intestine, pancreas, appendix, and diaphragm.

This is an expansive center, connecting you with the world around you, allowing you to take in experience and extend your own presence and influence outward.

With this chakra, there is an intake of impressions which creates a certain type of psychic attunement to what's going on around you, and is thus the source of gut feelings. *Manipura's* qualities are assimilation, personal presence, centeredness, confidence, and the solar aspects of cheerfulness, creativity and expansiveness. This is also a main area for generating, storing, and processing the flow of Life Force, or prana, within you.

You may visualize the vortex of energy being stimulated and generated in this area as a bright yellow flower opening its petals. Contract the muscles in this area, then gently relax them. Envision the column of energy drawn up into this solar plexus chakra. At the same time, effleurage your abdomen, which is to say, massage it in a circular motion. Feel the sensations generated in this area charging you with vitality and confidence. After you have concentrated on these sensations and images for several minutes, or whatever interval of time is comfortable, say aloud:

Joyfulness shines in me like a golden star,
like a golden sun within me.
Radiant energy flows through me.
I am a joyful spirit of light,
reveling in the lightness of my being.
Laughter comes easily from the depths of my belly.
I live welcoming to all experience.
I adventurously take part in the game of life,
and I have fun in everything I do.

Now, draw the column of energy upward in a spectrum transiting from golden yellow to yellow-green to a rich emerald green, to the heart chakra. This area includes the heart and thymus gland, as well as the lungs. It is known as *Anahata,* which is variously translated as "the unbeater" or "sound that is made without any two things striking."

Through this center, you are in attunement with the refined emotions of all your fellow beings, as well as the vibrations of higher spirits.

Activation of this center enhances our sense of relatedness. It puts one in sympathy with others, and hence has a psychic function in sending and receiving. The heart chakra's qualities are love, compassion, empathy, alignment, harmony, growth, healing, and regeneration. It is the balance point between mind, body, and spirit.

You may visualize the vortex of energy being stimulated and generated in this area as an intense green flower opening its petals. Lay your hands over this area. Experience the sensation of rich green energy pulsating in this area. Feel the emotions arising in this area filling you with pure, compassionate love that flows outward into the cosmos. After you have concentrated on these sensations and images for several minutes, or whatever interval of time is comfortable, say aloud:

I tread a path with heart,
*   celebrating the qualities of heart.*
I am open to all loving emotions,
*   and all healing emotions.*
My heart is open to all other hearts.
I give love freely, I receive love freely.
The quality of my love is ever growing,
*   and ever renewing.*

Now, draw the visualized energy upward, just as breath is drawn upward, in a spectrum transiting from green to blue-green to light aqua blue, to the throat chakra. This area is generally represented as centered in the hollow of the throat and includes the breathing apparatus upward of the lungs, the thyroid and parathyroid glands, the sinuses, and the mouth and speaking apparatus. It is known as *Visuddha,* which means purity or purification.

Through this center, you are connected with your ethereal body as well as the Akashic (ethereal) realm, as Visuddha *processes the intake of ethereal breath as well as oxygen. This chakra is a source of creativity because it enables us to transform our inner visions into outward forms of expression.*

Visuddha's qualities are communication, creative and artistic expression, resonance, transmutation, oxygenation, and the release of emotions and stress through speaking, sighing, laughing, and singing. *Visuddha* is the center where inner vision and sublime inspiration are transformed into outward expression. In a person of integrity, this chakra will be balanced so that person speaks with truth and sincerity.

Visualize this power center as a luminous flower, blending tones of light blue and aqua, opening its petals. Be especially aware of your breath as it passes through this area. Visualize currents of light blue and aqua coursing gently, but rhythmically, through this area. Focus on this area as you draw your breath through your body, breathing slowly and rhythmically. After you have concentrated on these sensations and images for several minutes, or whatever interval is comfortable, say aloud:

I express myself freely and openly.
I laugh, and laughter resonates throughout my being.
I sing, and the world is filled with song.
I breathe freely and deeply, for I am a free spirit,
        and lightness is my nature.
I fly over the Earth, touching blue skies,
        soaring in the realms of inspiration.

Now, draw your awareness upward to your brow chakra, visualizing a spectrum transiting from aqua to light blue to darker blue to the deep purplish blue which is indigo. This area includes your eyes, forehead, and that area between the eyes which is spoken of as the third eye (associated with the pineal gland), the pituitary gland, which balances your body's hormones, and to some extent your brain, nose, and ears. It is known as *Ajna,* which is variously translated as "to perceive" or "to command." It is sometimes called the Master Chakra because it is represented as the seat of the mind, directing the other chakras.

This center bridges the Conscious and Unconscious realms. Through it, you are connected with both inner and outer realities. Ajna's *qualities are clear perception, the appreciation of beauty, consciousness, intelligence, thought (and Higher Thought), the free flow of creative ideas, memory, wisdom, intuition, psychic vision, and dreams.*

Visualize this power center as a vibrant indigo blue flower opening its petals. Focus on this zone as you heighten your awareness. After you have concentrated on these sensations and images for several minutes, or whatever interval of time is comfortable, say aloud:

> *I look around me, seeing the beauty*
> *   and enchantment that fills my world.*
> *I look inside me and see bright fantasies*
> *   and visions of wonder.*
> *My ideas are templates for reality,*
> *   and reality is shaped in my imagining.*
> *I dream deep dreams of mystery and beauty.*
> *And I am one with the dreaming*
> *   of all living things.*

Finally, direct your attention to the crown chakra, that area which is represented as being at the top and to the back of your head, visualizing the energy moving in a spectrum from indigo to violet. The crown chakra shares some of the same areas as the brow chakra, including the pineal gland and the brain. However, its area also extends beyond your physical body, reaching into the ethereal realms to a transpersonal point that is outside of the physical. It is known as *Sahasrara,* which means "thousandfold." In art, it is depicted as a thousand-petaled lotus.

This center connects the individual's mind to the mind of the living Universe, creating an entrance point for spiritual and cosmic energies.

Sahasrara's qualities are religious feeling, deep spiritual understanding, Higher Thought and Knowledge, extended awareness, and oneness with the spirit of the Universe.

Visualize this power center as a deep purple or rich violet flower opening its petals. Focus your awareness on this zone, both where it is connected to your crown, and to where it extends outside of you—think of this as a halo. Visualize your energy extending outward and Cosmic Energy flowing inward, like a fountain flowing between you and the Universe. After you have concentrated on these sensations and images for several minutes, or whatever interval of time is comfortable, say aloud:

My life is suffused with wonder,
enriched by its spiritual dimension.
There is mystery and magic everywhere;
even in the smallest things,
even in the simplest things.
My mind, body, and spirit are one
with the Universal Being, nourished
by the spirit of the Living Universe.
I exult in my Oneness as the Higher Energies
flow through me.

Upon finishing this final visualization, sit in meditation, taking in the rich variety of sensations, impressions, and inspirations you will have aroused. As is usual with meditation, you will know when you have passed enough time with this. The images will begin to fade, and you will phase over into your normal waking state of consciousness, though much enriched and refreshed.

Although doing this type of exercise can put you in greater attunement with your surroundings, people, and the events of the moment, you should be able to go about your normal business afterwards; the chakras will just revert to whatever state is normal for you. If you should find yourself overly sensitized, you can undo the chakra exercise simply by visualizing the colors becoming more muted, or by going through the exercise in reverse order, visualizing the chakras as colored flowers closing their petals.

You can make the above chakra stimulation exercise more elaborate by incorporating it into larger meditation and study sessions, contemplating the physical, psychological, and spiritual associations of each chakra. If you wish to learn more about the chakra system, there are many books available which go into detail on this subject.[4] Also, this exercise would be suitable for a group meditation, if one person volunteers to read the text aloud, allowing the others to relax and focus on the visualizations.

Endnotes

1. Chakra systems can differ somewhat, though generally not greatly. The one provided here is fairly basic.

2. Shirley MacLaine's book, *Going Within, A Guide for Inner Transformation,* offers some especially good insights into how working with one's chakras can make a difference (New York: Bantam, 1989).

3. I will be presenting an intensified version of this Chakra Stimulation Exercise in my next book, *Moon Spells for Health and Wholeness.*

4. Some sources of reference on chakras include: Judith, Anodea, *The Truth About Chakras* and *Wheels of Life* (St. Paul: Llewellyn, 1990); Sherwood, Keith, *Chakra Therapy for Personal Growth and Healing* (St. Paul: Llewellyn, 1989); and Sui, Choa Kok, *Pranic Healing* (York Beach: Weiser, 1987).

Chapter 6

Creating Your Own
Magical Realm

With the help of magical fantasy, you can turn the mundane world around you into your own enchanted domain. Here, the word "magical" is used to mean that which is numinous, something that makes us feel that we can step outside of ordinary waking reality. As for fantasy, my dictionary defines it as "the free play of creative imagination," as well as "the power, process, or result of creating mental images modified by need, wish, or desire." So you could say that magical fantasy is the art of using imagination or imagery to make touch with the numinous.

For the purposes of the exercises in this chapter, the trick is for you to use your imagination, as well as your intuition, to sense magical potentials and to infuse places and things with magical imagery, animation, and meaning. Thus, your neighborhood, town, or county becomes your own fairy tale kingdom or queendom. An ancient gnarled tree becomes a wise old sentinel, protecting your realm. An interesting rock outcropping becomes a sleeping dragon. A large, flat boulder, perhaps dropped by a retreating glacier, becomes a wishing stone that you can stand on as you make a wish. The abandoned remains of a factory become the ruins of an ancient temple. A secluded glade in the local nature park becomes an elfin dancing place. You get the picture.

There are a number of genuine benefits from engaging in what may seem like a silly fantasy. To fantasize about a place is to claim it as your own territory. This attitude helps set you up for serendipitous situations because, if you're the KING or QUEEN, PRINCE or PRINCESS, then it follows that everything is there for you, that

everything you need will automatically be provided, in addition to being an affirmation of your personal power.[1]

Although a lot of this involves pure fantasy, a certain part is going to be based on listening to your intuition, and accepting what it says about people, places, and things, thus bringing you into greater attunement with your world, and with your Inner Knowing. Giving free reign to playful fantasies also brings you into attunement with Hermes, who, according to Combs and Holland, is:

> ...lord of the imagination as it comes like a gift from beyond the borders of the conscious mind. Allowing our imagination to play, letting our fantasies have their day, is to honor him.[2]

And to honor him is to be at one with the source of one's own creativity.

Bear in mind that, through the use of fantasy, you automatically project psychic energy into certain sites. If the appearance or ambience of certain places is such that other people unconsciously project meaning into them, then over time, they will indeed become magically active spots.

Projecting fantasy into special places can also lead us into deeper mysteries. In her work *The Dove in the Stone, Finding the Sacred in the Commonplace,* author Alice O. Howell gives us a glimpse into an imaginary land she created as a child.[3] Although Howell's imaginary world was an inner landscape of the mind, rather than a fantasy projected into her mundane environment, she shares an insight which is also relevant to attaching fantasies to your surroundings for purposes of playful magic, commenting:

> Its very spontaneous existence strikes me as a possible parallel in children to what perhaps was experienced by early or primitive man in centuries past or Aborigines in present times, and which in a humble way is where we start our quest for the archetypal Kingdom of Heaven. That the wee folk dwelt in our land and angels and archangels or devas or houris dwell on the higher levels, seemed natural to me then and even now.

For the purposes of playful magic, there are actually two basic fantasies involved here: not merely that your world is a magical realm, but that it's YOUR realm. By seeing yourself as the king or queen of all you survey, you can feel more expansive, secure, and confident, affirming that everything is good in your world. I was first struck with this concept when reading *A Sand County Almanac* by naturalist Aldo Leopold, who published his environmental classic back in 1949.[4] Leopold's magical country was the world of Nature at the crack of dawn. He says:

> ...it is a fact, patent both to my dog and myself, that at daybreak I am the sole owner of all the acres I can walk over. It is not only boundaries that disappear, but also the thought of being bounded. Expanses unknown to deed or map are known to every dawn, and solitude, supposed no longer to exist in my county, extends on every hand as far as the dew can reach.

He goes on to describe how he enjoys observing the waking activities of all the birds, who he sees as denizens of his realm, and mentions how:

> At 3:30 A.M., with such dignity as I can muster of a July morning, I step from my cabin door, bearing in either hand my emblems of sovereignty, a coffee pot and notebook.

Although Leopold may not have been consciously trying to project fantasy into his surroundings, he certainly had an intuitive grasp of it. From his above journal entries, we can also see that magical fantasy doesn't have to be confined to the stuff of fairy tales. If castles, elves, and knights in shining armor aren't your cup of tea, there are lots of other types of fantasies. For example, when a friend of mine goes walking with her buddy, the two of them like to make up little stories about the people who live in the houses they pass—people who they don't know, but the character of whose houses strikes their imagination. You can build your fantasy on anything that strikes your fancy.

Exploring Your World

You will find that you can build playful fantasies around the places and things of Nature, as well as manufactured things such as houses, statues, and other structures. The things of Nature's world are likely to play an especially big part in many fantasies, but that will be treated more thoroughly in the next chapter. Bear in mind, however, that for the purposes of this chapter, discussion of places and things will cover both the natural and the artificial.

To go about assigning the landmarks and denizens of your own special realm, you can first use your intuition to tell you which places and things in your neighborhood might already carry a psychic charge. Such places may make you feel moody, dreamy, or tingly, or they may simply be "feel good" spots. It's

good to rely on your initial impressions, whatever jumps into your mind when viewing a certain site for the first time. When looking at familiar sites that you go by often, try to recall what might have gone through your mind the first time you saw them.

Next, you use intuition to pick up any additional insights, and your imagination to project special fantasies into those places and things. Also consider those places and things that look like they have the potential to play a part in your fantasy, even if you aren't able to psychically or intuitively sense anything from them.

As you start taking a closer look at things in you area, becoming aware of them for their fantasy potential, you'll notice that certain things can draw strong emotional responses from you, things that affect you positively, making you feel warm, sentimental, or energized. Of course, there can be things that get negative reactions, too. Sometimes you'll find a site that you really "connect" with—where you can feel a strong rapport. Bingo. You know you've found an especially magical place to include on your psychic map. Always be alert to your first impressions, as these are going to be the most significant.

In order to spin fantasies, it's important to not be hurried. Sometimes you just have to be willing to loiter around. Some types of fantasies can come with familiarity. You may find that you are more likely to make sentimental or psychic attachments to the places that you have been passing repeatedly over a number of years. Get to know the areas you frequent through all your senses. While you're lingering in a place, close your eyes to hear subtle sounds, breathe in through your nostrils to become more aware of the characteristic odors, run your hands across natural and manufactured objects to feel their texture, observe colors and patterns, you can even try to taste the air to familiarize yourself with the character of a place. Also, anything you can do to learn more about local and natural history will add to your appreciation of your environs, adding richness and texture to your world, even if it doesn't specifically relate to your personal fantasies.

Getting back to the concept of animism discussed in Chapter 2, when you develop a relationship with the things in your world, you start perceiving their personalities. To create your fantasies, you may find it helpful to reach back into your own childhood memories and resurrect the types of fantasies or impressions you had about places and things. If you live in a new place, you can project those old fantasies into your new surroundings.

If you have lived in your area for some time, there are probably some places that have sentimental meanings for you because some good memories have been made there. From studies of applied kinesiology, we know that places that have positive mental associations for you strengthen you physically as well as emotionally— even just by thinking of them. Naturally, you'll want to give these places a role of honor in your private fantasy province.

If you happen to live in the same house or town where your ancestors have lived, or otherwise have access to places they visited regularly or carried out their daily activities, then these places are likely to have special resonance for you. Such places give you a chance to link with your own ancestral dreaming time.

By the way, when looking at people, places, and things that strike some kind of chord in us, it can be difficult to separate what is the result of a psychological response from what comes from the psychic senses. Of course, psychological and psychical factors often go hand in hand, and it's likely you're tuning into a variety of different energies which may be there for whatever reasons. However, we're not concerned with separating psychology from psychism here, we're just concerned about the fantasy.

Projecting the Fantasy

Sometimes you just can't pick anything up from your surroundings, psychically or intuitively, either because you're not strongly intuitive (which just means you haven't developed your sense of intuition), or maybe it's a place that truly doesn't have much resonance. If you can't find enough places that you instinctively respond to, then you might have to more consciously apply imagination to come up with fantasies for places and things. As mentioned, consciously projecting fantasy into a place or thing would give it a real psychic charge over a period of time. When you fantasize about something, the attention you direct toward it automatically imbues it with a quality of energy which, for lack of a better description, I will refer to as psychic energy.

Projecting psychic energy into something, whether done consciously or unconsciously, gives it a special strength. If it's a place or thing that has a special function in your fantasy world, such as a dreaming place or wishing place, then it heightens the quality of what you would experience there.

It is possible to create a psychic charge or intensify the existing power of a place or thing: If you feel that your contribution of energy will be welcomed by the thing or the Spirit of Place, stand before the spot in a calm, meditative state of mind, breathing deeply and rhythmically. Visualize that the atmosphere around you has become alive, with every inch of space being shot through with shimmering silver sparkles, each one a spark of cosmic energy. Maintain this visualization for as long as you can. When you can no longer maintain the visualization or whenever you feel the psychic charge has "taken," just throw a kiss in the direction of the area in question, then turn away and go on about your business. Psychic charging has no negative effects since it really amounts to giving an area or a thing a Life Force tonic. It can actually nourish the people, plants, and animals around it.

The Focus of Fantasy

Certain types of places and things that can often be found in ordinary neighborhoods are able to generate, attract, and/or accumulate psychic energy by their nature, appearance, or function. There is a whole body of literature written about how nature spots are viewed as sacred or powerful in natural energy (this will be touched on in chapter 7). Different kinds of structures can also lend themselves to individual fantasies. Some things that especially have a way of becoming focal points for psychic energy in a community are statues, bridges, piers, lighthouses, bell towers, flagpoles, fountains (even drinking fountains), band shells, gazebos, abandoned buildings, and buildings with historical significance, architectural interest, or a long tradition of importance to the community. Cemeteries have a lot of sentiment and superstition bound up in them. I've noticed they are strong reservoirs of Earth energy, perhaps because of the placement of stone monuments and the fact that lots of birds and animals can live there undisturbed, in addition to the human emotions that are poured out there.

The design of certain structures and places also has the ability to capture the imagination. Features of buildings and houses such as windows, doors, stairs, fireplaces, and chimneys, and features of private and public gardens, such as fences, gateways, arbors, and meandering pathways can suggest fantasy elements.

In surveying your neighborhood, you may find that some ordinary residences elicit positive psychic and emotional responses. People consciously and unconsciously funnel a lot of energy into their material environment. Therefore, plain suburban homes and gardens can be pretty active psychically. This is especially true of homes which show a strong amount of owner pride, devotion, and individuality, as well as signs that the occupants share a lot of "heart activities" and enjoy a quality emotional life. This can be more noticeable if the residents go to lengths to celebrate and decorate for holidays. Sometimes homes that seem to have the "magic touch" may not be anything special—you can't tell whether it's something in the way they're built or decorated, or just something in the way it's all put together, or something else. When I'm on a walk, those kinds of homes tend to catch my attention, and I feel grateful to the occupants for putting the good vibes into the neighborhood. If more households consciously worked to create this sort of ambience, it would surely restore life to a lot of depressed areas. It would also help deter crime, since crooks are intimidated by places that give off a strong sense of people-presence.

Special Uses for
Special Places

In establishing the extent of your fantasy domain, you'll find that some of the most important places are ones that do something for you. Whether these spots are nature parks or buildings and other artificial creations, there are places that can make you feel happy, places that call up memories and deep sentiments, places that energize you (sometimes by absorbing your negativity and then recharging you), and places that stir your creative powers. Some of these will be places where you go to think, to get inspired ideas, to relax, to let go of negative emotion, to be alone with the creatures of nature, to interact with other people, or to watch the world go by. It's interesting that children's literature can give us ideas for spots that are therapeutic or have personal meaning, such as Winnie-the-Pooh's "thinking spot" and Brer Rabbit's "laughin' place."

If you have favorite affirmations that you like to say, you may find that there are different places in your area where it feels especially good or appropriate to do them. For example if there's some particular thing or quality that you're trying to affirm, such as love, prosperity, happiness, or peace, you might find that certain areas inspire you more to affirm certain things. It's also nice to give blessings. This involves sending good wishes to the things you see that please you or that you feel need a good energy booster. You can do this simply by looking at the object in question and mentally saying, "Blessings." If you pass a place with an aura of depression, you can mentally envision sunbeams reaching into its darkest corners, like soft caressing fingertips.

If you're lucky, there may also be some spots that have a particularly strong mystical quality. Such places can be Wishing Places, Dreaming Places, and points where you feel you can step into another world altogether.

The site that you feel is imbued with the greatest magical power, or at least has the most emotional appeal enabling you to project a lot of psychic energy or fantasy into it, can become a Wishing Place. As implied, this is where you can go to make wishes, as well as say special affirmations about things that you feel are out of reach (see Appendix IV, *Affirmations*). When you're at your Wishing Place, accept that you're in the presence of a Higher Power that can make anything come true. However, in accordance with the suggestions in Chapter 3, it would be a good idea to first make wishes for things that are on your secondary goals list, things that do not have a lot of emotional desperation attached to them, as even Wishing Places might need to be primed for a good start. Incidentally, your Wishing Place doesn't have to be a "place" as such, it can be a thing, such as an ancient tree, a stone lion whose nose you can rub for luck, or a large, flat boulder you can stand upon while wishing.

A Dreaming Place is a place of vision, an isolated, quiet spot where you can relax, even lay down, while you clear your mind to meditate and receive dreams, visions, and inspirations. Like the Wishing Place, it should be a site where you sense a very strong magical and mystical potential, but it's important that it be an area where you can have complete solitude, a place set apart from the world, a place where you feel protected. Such an area is also likely to have a strong sense of the past, and may be a spot that was significant to early settlers and Native Americans before them.

You may be able to find some areas that are so secluded, or exotic, or wild in appearance that you get the feeling that you've gone through a portal into another dimension, and are in another world altogether. It can be like a fantasy world within your fantasy world. You are most likely to get this sensation when, in order to get to the spot, it's necessary to pass through or between something—underbrush, hanging vines, branches, narrow rock walls—to enter some especially isolated site. Sometimes the primal quality of such a place can make you feel like you're going back into the time of the dinosaurs or entering alien terrain, even some parks in the heart of the city can have hidden glades with that unearthly atmosphere. Of course, such a site could serve as your Wishing place or Dreaming Place—a nexus point where two worlds meet.

Additional Things
to Do

Although some places can serve a purpose for you such as a Wishing Place or Dreaming Place, your fantasy sites don't always have to have a function and you don't always have to do something when you visit them. Some may be places you just acknowledge or appreciate. In fact, some may be sites you don't even have access to, that are only viewed from afar or viewed in passing.

To reinforce the fantasy that you're surveying your own magical kingdom or queendom, you can create special visualizations for places and things. For example, you can use your imagination to translate the things you view into the fairy tale imagery mentioned earlier or employ any other images to enhance your personal fantasies, which could be a tropical paradise, a mountaintop Shangrila, or any number of things. If you need ideas to help you create a fantasy framework, listen to what neighborhood children say about places and things: What do they think they look like? What special names do they have for them? You can also use affirmations to support the fantasy such as, "I live in a world of magic," or "My empire is vast and beautiful."

It's always nice to have personal greetings for both the animate and inanimate objects inhabiting your realm. This can include words and gestures like hugging a tree, saluting a statue, whistling to the birds, as well as secret codes and signals known only to you.

It's also quite appropriate to leave offerings as gestures of appreciation at special places. An offering can be a simple courtesy—a way of showing respect to both the earthly and otherworldly inhabitants of the place. Shiny pennies and polished stones make good offerings, as well as substances that can be consumed by animals or returned to nature, such as flowers, wreaths, and sprinkled grain or cornmeal.

Once you've developed your fantasy fairly well, you might want to create a magical trek. Lay out a special trail or route where, by walking or driving, you can make a circuit of most of your favorite sites. In making a regular pilgrimage, you lay down a circuit of psychic energy, building a protective circle around your world.

Charting the Fantasy

If you enjoy putting things on paper, it can be fun to make a map of your magical realm, or at least a small part of it, such as your immediate neighborhood or favorite nature park. Such a map realistically depicts the physical environment (unlike the type of map suggested in Chapter 10, where you chart an imaginary utopia), but you tag magical significance to certain things and places.

In labeling your map, be sure to write any fantasy attributes or magical meanings into the titles and symbols on the map's legend. If you have developed a route for your magical trek, outline it. You might orient the map by deciding which place will be at the "center" of your world. For most of us, it would be natural for this to be our home, though some may feel that way about their school, work, or other favorite hang-outs. What you choose to designate as the center can give you some insight into your Self. What you choose to designate as the borderlands can also give you insight into your personal boundaries. As you look over your map taking in the big picture, see if any interesting patterns emerge. Does the layout of anything suggest geometric forms or runic symbols? All these things can be magically or psychologically significant. Be sure to note personal comments and reminisces of good times that have been had in various places, such as "This is where the kids and I saw seven swans swim past." If you're not a good artist, you can note these things down on an already existing map. Nature parks usually provide trail maps that show various features.

Personal Space

After putting all of this thought into picking up impressions and projecting fantasy into the places around you, you'll naturally find you can apply the same principles to the most obvious place—your home. When you have a place of your own, the advantage is that you have a certain amount of control over your surroundings, so you can decorate and arrange things to suit your fantasies and set the mood for magic. The things around you can reflect your inner state, but rearranging your outer world influences the inner being, so they can also affect it. There are many things you can do to make your environment more friendly to spontaneity, free expression, flexibility, humor, play, and magic. Some of the changes you can make are fairly simple: surround yourself with things that cheer you such as sun catchers and objects of natural beauty, things that pleasantly engage your five senses, that display your sense of humor, and that are life-affirming. The use of mood-altering items such as lighting, candles, incense, and music can define personal space as something magical, set apart from the world.

You can project unique fantasy elements into common household items, just as with the things in your wider world, as discussed earlier. Features of your house such as stair cases, cellars, attics, closets, and fireplaces, or furniture items such as mirrors, musical instruments, comfy chairs, old trunks, old photos, and other interesting antiques such as grandfather clocks can all lend themselves to your imagination. If you are an animist who sees distinctive personalities in inanimate objects, it's with your household objects that you're most likely to develop such a relationship.

If possible, consider creating private spaces where you feel you're stepping outside of the mundane world and into a world of your own. A desire to bring fantasy into the home can get fairly elaborate: some people like to devote whole rooms of their house to a certain fantasy. This is a kind of escapism that really relieves stress. Usually this is built around a hobby such as doll collecting or model trains. (Incidentally, there's magical significance to such hobbies, which will be discussed in Chapter 11.) Some of these fantasies recreate enchanted memories from childhood—such as the sense of wonder a child may feel when looking at a Christmas fantasy toy display in the illuminated window of a department store. Other fancies that people indulge when decorating special rooms include: ships' cabins, historical reconstructions, courtesans' boudoirs, Middle Easter seraglios, etc. Garden fantasies can also be used to restore the soul, decked out as tropical paradises, zen meditation gardens, magical grottos, and other Shangri-las. Naturally, gratifying these kinds of whims requires having adequate space and the financial wherewithal.

Sharing the Fantasy

The type of fantasies described here can be discussed with understanding family members and with friends who are kindred spirits. When you're with such persons, you feel that you're in a safe place, that you can repeat your wild ideas or visions to them without worrying about being viewed as weird or being ridiculed. There's a special joy to be had, and you'll discover an amazing thing: sharing a fantasy will put you "in sync" with each other. You'll be surprised at how you intuitively start experiencing some of the same thoughts, dreams, and inspirations.

Some Individual
Fantasies

It's not unusual for normal people to have elements of magical fantasy in their lives. Although these fantasies might not be as elaborate as the creation of the invisible empire we've discussed in this chapter, they can revolve around the places and things that people interact with. Here are some examples that have been related to me by friends and family.

The most frequently mentioned fantasies or intuitive impressions seem to center on trees—especially coming from people who find comfort in hugging trees. My friend, Judy M. says that whenever she returns to her family farm, she visits a special oak tree that is her source of inspiration. Her family has noticed this, and has taken to calling it Judy's tree. She's also feels a sense of reverence at a stand of pine trees which form a "cathedral" around a pond. The cathedral-like atmosphere of certain woods seems to make an impression on lots of different people. Beth M., also a tree-hugging aficionado, has a hugging tree in her backyard which comforts her when she's feeling low. She says, "It's a special friend I can talk to." This particular tree is hardy, even in droughts. Cats, as well as other people, pick up on it and are attracted to it. Beth says that visitors will often comment, "Gee, what did you do to that tree?" When you're really attracted to a certain tree, it's natural to perceive its personality and include it as an important denizen of your fantasy world.

Among manufactured objects, automobiles are the ones most likely to develop animistic qualities. People give their cars names and personalities, and feel that they last longer and work better as a result. Cars and other objects that are related to in this way are less likely to fall victims to our throw-away society, so there's an ecological ethic here.

Sometimes people can create objects with fantasies attached to them. My dad likes to make "stick people" on a wilderness beach

in the north by standing interesting logs, sticks, and pieces of drift-wood upright in the sand. He says that he thinks about them, wondering what happens to them during the day or night. He finds they also have a protective quality, acting as sentinels or tikis. He's always very pleased on the occasions when he returns to the beach and finds them still standing after a hard winter.

When Nancy P. moved into her first house, standing near the pool there was a large, round boulder that somewhat resembled an

Easter Island figure, or a large stone tiki, with features suggesting a face with an open mouth. Nancy and her husband and kids called him La La, enhanced his face slightly with a drill, and put candles in his mouth. The whole family sensed that La La had protective powers, and they thought of him as an assistant life-guard, keeping watch over the pool. Certain strangers would actually find him somewhat fearsome and frightening, while party guests would often leave offerings of food in front of him.

Beth M., the aforementioned tree hugger, also has a special friendship with the San Gabriel River, visualizing its spirit as The Lady of the River. She says, "I always greet her in crossing, so she knows I do love her and appreciate her. It makes me feel good to greet her." Incidentally, the Lady also gives Beth a helping hand. Beth and a commuting companion have to drive along a particularly congested route near the river and when they find themselves in a traffic jam, they call on the Lady, who always manages to make an opening for them. This recognition of the spirit of place has also helped Ann T., who experienced major culture shock when she moved from the greenness of northern California to the congestion of Los Angeles. When she learned the city was named in honor of Our Lady, the Queen of the Angels, she was able to connect with the presence of the Lady and thus be more reconciled with the place, even though she herself is not a Catholic.

Morgana MacArthur, a writer in Santa Cruz, has a dragon who lives under her deck, but likes to spend a lot of time under her kitchen table. She initially got to know the fantasy dragon, named Draco, when she was living in a house on a forested mountaintop. Her four children picked up on it right away, sharing the fantasy and building on it. Sometimes one of the kids will take a crumb of food and lean under the table, hold it out and say, "I'm giving Draco a bite." When the family moved to the city, they were concerned whether Draco would want to come along. However, he soon showed up. Morgana says, "Draco is a casual, but accepted, part of our reality." She feels they can sense his presence and his

reactions, saying, "Frequently we close the door on his tail, and he lets us know about it!" The MacArthur family members have also observed that their cats and dog seemed upset at first about Draco's presence, but now have made their peace. The MacArthurs agree that a shared fantasy gives a family a special bond.

My own son has created a role-playing board game featuring our neighborhood set in an alternate, futuristic reality. His friends come over regularly to participate in this ongoing adventure, so there is a large number of kids becoming involved in the fantasy, and adding to it. People, animals, schools, houses, and shops are featured, and the kids are building quite a neighborhood mythology. Since they spend a lot of time drawing pictures and making maps of these things, they certainly have a greater level of geographical consciousness, which is something educators generally like to encourage. Also, their awareness of everyday things in the neighborhood is enhanced, and so is mine—I learn a lot from them.

Shelly, who has two contrary roles as an artist and a business-woman, has done the reverse of projecting anthropomorphic features into the landscape. She lives in a small town where she doesn't find many kindred spirits. She also has to deal with large segments of the general public on a regular basis. As anyone who deals with the public knows, a lot of people are very friendly and reasonable, but there are people out there who are just walking around looking for someone to vent their hostilities on. To help cope with all these different people, with all their different demands and energies, Shelly walks what she calls her "Faery Flower Path." She envisions her daily life as a garden path, and she perceives the people she encounters along the way as features of the natural landscape. Pleasant people are perceived as flowers and butterflies, the surly ones get shined on as rocks and other inert matter. Shelly says that to be reconciled with reality, you have to be "enough in touch to stay totally out of it." With those words of wisdom in mind, we'll close this chapter on fantasy.

Endnotes

1. For those readers who may object that this metaphor smacks of imperialism and exploitation, I want to emphasize that it is not meant to promote the idea of power over anything or anybody. Rather, it is a fantasy to promote personal empowerment, and loving attunement with all who share your world. It is assumed the reader will approach the physical and social environment with respect and sensitivity.

2. Combs, Allan, and Holland, Mark. *Synchronicity—Science, Myth, and the Trickster.* New York: Paragon House, 1990. Page 135.

3. Howell, Alice O. *The Dove in the Stone, Finding the Sacred in the Commonplace.* Wheaton: Theosophical Publishing House, 1988. Incidentally, when Howell visited the mystical isle of Iona, she was surprised to see its landscape paralleled the inner landscape of her childhood fantasies.

4. Leopold, Aldo. *A Sand County Almanac.* New York: Ballantine, 1984, originally 1949.

Chapter 7

The Magic of Nature

When I wrote the previous chapter on magical fantasy, I interviewed my friends on how they use intuition, magic, and creative imagination to enhance their daily lives. They all said their most meaningful meditations, fantasies, dreams and experiences come through entering into a playfully magical relationship with Nature. This is not surprising—touch with Nature is touch with magic.

When I use the word Nature, as I do in practically every other sentence in this chapter, I do so knowing that I cannot possibly define what Nature is. True, the word encompasses the physical features of the outdoors and the wilderness, the plants, animals, and their relationships in the wildlife community, but there is also that living spirit of Nature. This is the entity that has been so lovingly spoken of by poets, philosophers, geomancers, mystics, and shamans. Even persons with no mystical inclinations can relate to Mother Nature, and these days more people are be coming aware of Gaia or Gaea, the great Goddess, the Being of Planet Earth

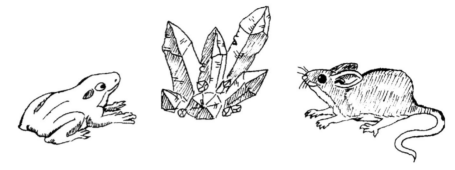

Herself, as the concern for her well-being is growing. For the purposes of this chapter, suffice it to say that Nature is alive—whether you perceive this entity as the Earth Mother, the Great Spirit, or by any other name or manifestation—and that She, He, or It has a playful spirit which reaches out to us in love and friendship.

A magical relationship with the spirit of Nature has genuine benefits for us—it allows us to experience true aliveness. Trees, rock formations, places with exposure to water, wind, or sunshine, and many of this world's other forms and forces are strong in prana, or ki, which is that energy we call the Life Force. It is essentially the same energy that is bound up with magical or psychical energy. One of the ways to experience this energy is through the use of magical fantasy, as mentioned previously, and it is also perceived when honoring, celebrating, and participating in the community of Nature and her creatures.

Of course, the magic of Nature isn't just about receiving personal benefits from Mother Nature, it's also about giving energy BACK to her. All of Earth's places are sacred, but many of them need our help to reverse the massive ecological despoliation that humans have inflicted. Approaching Nature with a playful, but respectful, spirit is one way to help revivify her.

Because the natural world is so vastly magical, I can barely scratch the surface of this subject in this limited space. However, I will share some of the following insights and provide some suggestions on playful relationship with Nature.

Observation and Awareness

One of the great advantages of being outdoors is that the conditions of Nature can encourage us to synthesize the conflicting modes of sensing and intuition.

In Jungian psychology (as discussed in Chapter 4), sensing and intuition refer to different ways of thinking about things, experiencing the world, and approaching reality. People who have a natural tendency toward the sensing mode notice details and accurately observe what is going on in the physical world. They are practical and concerned with the here and now. People who tend to be more intuitive are more concerned with possibilities and speculations, and live inside their heads. Their awareness is unfocused, simultaneously picking up on a variety of conflicting subliminal stimuli, but often failing to observe actual, physical details. One of the field marks of these types of people is that they have all kinds of old and new bruises on their bodies that they don't remember getting—especially at table, counter, and doorknob height—from bumping into things that they didn't notice.

We humans can more fully appreciate Nature if we learn to use our five senses to sharply distinguish all of the subtle activities, details, and changes that are going on at any given moment. Animals rely on this for survival. When out in the solitude and purity of the outdoors, we can also experience another dimension, where we perceive great undercurrents of unseen energies and apprehend what is going on below the surface even if we can't explain why. Some would say this is our touch with the Spirit World. The desirable goal is to be able to enjoy taking in Nature with all of our five senses while at the same time feeling connected, through other senses, to a larger unseen world.

There is a problem that intuitively-oriented people can experience when alone outdoors: they can fail to perceive the fullness and grandeur of wilderness if they should happen to get locked inside their own heads. If you have this particular problem, you sometimes don't perceive what is going on around you, and your intuitions can be false. Yes, just as a thinking person can be dead wrong in his or her analysis of things, so too can an intuitive person get locked inside a head that isn't generating any fresh thoughts or taking in any new information, whether from inner or outer sources. Old and unproductive thoughts are looping around inside your head, being rehashed, as you think about your personal concerns, the problems of the world, or the plot of the latest movie you saw, instead of being open to the vast world of sensation, beauty, and experience around you.

On the other hand, sensing types can be excellent observers of Nature's features and phenomena, and yet have no deeper bond or attunement with her Being, thus deriving no personal meaning or spiritual nourishment from a relationship with her.

I have found the works of Tom Brown to be the most helpful to me in trying to develop a greater awareness in rapport with the great spirit of Nature.[1] Brown is a naturalist who is well known as a tracker, and has written a large number of books on tracking and nature observation, wilderness survival, and Earth-honoring philosophy and spirituality. Brown's teachings synthesize the qualities of observation and intuition. Relating the teachings he learned from his childhood mentor, Stalking Wolf, an Apache scout, tracker, stalker, healer, and shaman, Brown offers some very effective techniques for improving attention and observation and practicing conscientious survivalism as a doorway toward entering the world of Spirit and knowing the presence of The Spirit that Moves Through All Things. Brown says:

> The deeper significance of survival extends far beyond the simple feat of knowing how to stay alive in the wilderness... With the practice of survival one begins to relax into the Earth, to learn its rhythms, to blend in balance and harmony with all things. Survival, as a way of life, removes man from the sterility of society and brings him to a hand-to-mouth

existence with the Earth. He begins to understand what the ancients understood: that Earth is Mother, and we can never live without her. Because all things of the Earth—people, animals, insects, plants—are from one Mother, we must realize that we are all brothers and sisters in a real way.[2]

Brown's teachings emphasize the "purity" of Wilderness, and I find that when I'm out in Nature, but losing focus and going into the loops inside of my head, remembering Brown's explanations of that word, "purity," acts as a mantra, or key, to bring me back into a focused awareness that phases into rapture.

Whatever techniques or paths you follow in developing wilderness appreciation and observation, exploring the world of Nature is certainly one of the best ways of integrating the whole person. The methods offered by Tom Brown and other naturalists are a rich resource available to you. One technique Brown emphasizes is called "Splatter Vision." It is used by native Americans to spot game, and by animals to spot danger. Brown explains:

It is done by simply looking toward the horizon and allowing your vision to "spread out." In other words, instead of focusing on a single object, allow the eyes to soften and take in everything in a wide half sphere. The effect is like putting a wide-angle lens on a camera. Suddenly your vision is greatly increased. Everything in your "viewfinder" is a little fuzzy because your eyes are not focused, but they are much more sensitive to movement. To identify a movement, all you have to do is focus on it.[3]

Rely on your intuition to suggest new techniques for shifting and focusing your awareness. Try experimenting with modes of awareness using your various senses. For example, go into a hearing mode: listen to sounds your feet are making, then shift to bird sounds, wind sounds, street sounds, etc., then open yourself to hearing the entire chorus of sounds in symphony. You can also try this with your senses of vision, smell, and touch. (By the way, this hearing mode is important to Patricia Ancona Ha, an artist who draws inspiration from communication with the voices of animals, plants, and stones. She says, "Receptivity to the energy of an area comes from paying attention and learning to listen to what lives there." She is now teaching this ability to her four-year-old.)

Of course, you'll discover the value of cultivating the two most important modes of all: patience and silence. Learn to watch and sit silently, calm all mental static, and put aside all sense of time. If you're out with friends, learn to feel comfortable with mutual silence, agree to dispense with trivial chatter. Turn off the judging function which always has to have a product or a purpose or a result, and tune into the openness and flow of the perceiving function. Take the same attitude as Henry David Thoreau, who said, "Time is but the stream I go a-fishing in."

As an awareness expansion exercise, consider the following technique, which I call "Winged Spirit," celebrating the flight and freedom of birds. Whatever birds do, they always seem to be at play. We can especially envy them the gift of flight, because soaring above trees and houses gives them a special perspective on the world around us. The following exercise is a way of using your imagination to view the world the way a may bird see it, as well as experiencing the fantasy of flight.

Winged Spirit: An Exercise in Imaginative Sensation

Stand outdoors or relax on a flat stone or park bench in an area frequented by different varieties of birds. Birds tend to be most active in the morning. Around 10:00 A.M. is a good time to watch them, because the angle of the sun is favorable. Be alert but at ease. Spend some time just observing the birds—noticing their distinct physical differences, characteristic actions, body language and movements, and so on. After you have genuinely become absorbed in observing the birds' activities, empty your mind of any

intrusive thoughts. Breathe deeply and slowly. Open your awareness to all of the sensations of the natural world around you. Feel
the sun and the breeze caressing your skin. Drink in the smell of
the flowers and plants. Listen to all of the bird songs, as well as the
other sounds around you.

Now, direct your attention specifically to the birds. Don't close
your eyes, but do relax your eyelids. With your fingers, press gently on your temples. Reach out with your mind. Visualize yourself
as one of their flock. While you are doing this, generate thoughts
of sunlight, warmth, peace, and well-being, so that if your mind
does happen to touch that of the birds, they will not be alarmed. As
the birds fly from one tree or rooftop to another, or hop from
branch to branch, hold these emotions in your mind.

When you feel you've achieved a strong rapport with the bird energies, you may close your eyes, sit back, and allow any sensations that you pick up to flow into you.

Bird energies will be quite different from what you're used to, but allow your consciousness to flow with them. Experience these energies with a whole-body awareness. Open your mind to all of the sensations that birds may feel, and the images that they may see. These images and sensations may seem distorted to you, but let them flow. Experience the sheer exaltation of flight, soaring now higher, now lower. Revel in the sensation of being feathered and of moving rapidly and joyously through the cool air. Sense the variety of breezes, currents, and thermals that make up the medium in which the bird so freely moves.

After a few moments, gently withdraw your consciousness, pulling yourself back to your normal waking state. Open your eyes and stretch your body, making yourself aware of your own flesh and bones. Later, as you go through your day, you might consider whether having seen things in a new way affects your own perception of familiar sights.

Interacting with Nature

Along with developing observation and awareness, there are little things we can do to enable us to interact playfully with Mother Earth and her creatures.

One of the most popular means by which a human can extend warm and loving feelings is through tree hugging. Tree hugging has become a cliche used derisively by people who like to make fun of ecologists and New Agers, but it is the practice most commonly cited by my friends and many others. Relating to the spirits of trees is such a meaningful experience, it should come as no surprise this isn't just some new fad. Consider the following anecdote from *Myths and Legends of Flowers, Trees, Fruits, and Plants:*

In Tusculum the hill of Corne was covered with beeches, curiously round like evergreens in a topiarian's garden, and dedicated to Diana, to worship whom the people came from miles around; and one of these trees was a favorite of the orator Passenius Crispus, who read and meditated in its shade, embraced it familiarly, and often testified to his regard by pouring wine on its roots.[4]

It's odd, sometimes, how the old patterns of Earth honoring come through spontaneous remembering of forgotten traditions. I remember an occasion when I was a youngster, standing around with a bunch of other kids at a Sunday School picnic: we were all ceremoniously pouring our sodas onto the ground in respectful libation to the Earth. Where did we get such an idea? It's certainly not something encouraged in Sunday School.

Large and small acts of consideration, rites of honoring and blessing, these are ways of bringing oneself into attunement with Nature's greater energies, including her playful energies. Such an example is cited by Robert Lawlor in *Voices of the First Day: Awakening in the Aboriginal Dreamtime.* He says:

> I once visited a huge standing rock formation at sunset, in a glowing red canyon outside Sedona, Arizona, with a man of the Cherokee tribe, Willy Whitefeather. When we arrived, he sat down directly facing the stones and played a lilting melody on his flute. Later, he said that stones have silicone crystals inside them, through which they listen! "They are like lonely old people, standing and waiting to be sung to. Our people have always sung songs of admiration to the qualities of strength, beauty, and endurance that stones bring into our world...They are tired and lonely now because the white world has become so blind and selfish. They live in a hollow unsung world."[5]

In Chapter 4, we touched on the subject of elemental spirits, entities that are manifestations of the elements of Fire, Earth, Water, and Air. The authors and psychics who have studied and

worked with elementals have always commented on their high energy and playfulness. Interaction with them is uniquely exhilarating. To get to know the elemental spirits, you start by getting to know their element. For example,observe how elemental Water manifests in the world of Nature around you—not merely in the obvious things like lakes and rivers, but in other things like moisture in the air, sap in trees, or the lifeblood of people and animals. Consider its actions, whether in flowing, carrying, penetrating, nourishing, or eroding. Then, meditate on how this element is at work within you, and how its power expresses itself in your nature. With the soul essence of your own being, make a relationship with the soul essence of the element—elementals are experienced when the spirit of humanity touches the spirit of Nature.

Similarly, it's possible to reach out to the other forms and manifestations of Nature's intelligence and imagination, often referred to as the devas, spirits of rocks and plants and animals, even those entities we call the Spirits of Place. Such contacts are generally subtle and intuitive, not dramatic enough to write about in a magazine of amazing true adventures, but meaningful and sublime enough to alter the way you see and approach the environment.

Incidentally, in the Old World it was common to perceive elementals and nature spirits in more human forms, the way we might image the kobolds, dryads, and undines, whereas Native Americans tended to identify them in more purely animal forms. This has also been the experience of myself and friends when sensing their presence. It makes sense. Europe and Asia have been more densely populated over a long period of time and human resonance has built up there, so the nature spirits gained more of an air of familiarity (at least from the human point of view), and hence more human form. However, in approaching American wilderness sites, the animal forms are more likely to be encountered, as we have not yet left a lasting imprint on these places.

For more ideas on interacting with the features and creatures of nature, you can incorporate some of the techniques suggested in the previous chapter, which include using intuition and imagination to detect "feel good" spots and other places that carry a magical charge or mystical quality, getting to know places intimately and learning their history, appreciating the sense of just being there with no purpose or product in mind, projecting warm greetings to the local inhabitants (whether animal, plant, mineral, or spiritual), and leaving offerings that will nourish or replenish the animals and the environment.

The previous chapter also mentioned creating a mindset of being in your own magical realm—this encompasses the world of Nature where you live. There is an ecological ethic inherent in this, because the conscientious person sees his or her role as a friend and steward of the local wildlife population. This means seeing oneself as a member of the community of rocks, plants, and animals, honoring them as your good neighbors, or as the Ojibwa do, our elder brothers and sisters. Here, it is important to appreciate all of your animal friends, even the common ants, sparrows, and squirrels, not just the animals that most people think are "cool," such as hawks, eagles, wolves, mountain lions, or dolphins.

Always bear in mind that an important part of honoring the natural community is leaving it alone and respecting the privacy of its other inhabitants whenever and wherever appropriate. Consider the Lakota Indians, who would set apart special places they would avoid or leave undisturbed, because they believed the animals needed to have some place to do their own sacred ceremonies.

Magical Places

Playful interaction with Nature can lead to a recognition of the Spirit of Place, as well as to a rapport with the Earth energies.

There has been a surge of interest in Sacred Places, and this ties in with a lot of fascinating geomantic theories about the Life Force or Earth Spirit as it flows through landforms, structures, things, and places.[6] As you might expect, most of this interest focuses on the more dramatic geological forms and historically important religious sites. These places are felt to have the strongest concentration of prana and magic, and people are flocking to them for renewal, healing, vision, and personal transformation.[7]

If you are like most of the population, you're not likely to have a volcano, a waterfall, or even a Stonehenge in your urban or suburban neighborhood. Even when there are natural power spots near you, accessibility is apt to be a problem if they're on private property. That doesn't mean that your ordinary neighborhood is devoid of Nature's magic. Using intuition and magical fantasy, you can look for places in your area that have magical energy and potential. There are natural features that may be found in some neighborhood parks, woodlots, or other fringe areas, or even in certain public places. Places where you can have meaningful interaction with the environment may include:

- places where you notice a high level of animal activity or an interesting selection and arrangement of plant life

- trees, landforms, and rock outcroppings of age and character

- natural springs, where water trickles out of the earth

- places where nature has shaped a comfortable ledge or seat for sitting in meditation, like a flattened boulder

- natural amphitheaters or small openings in a park or forest which strike you as potential dance or ceremonial places

- grottos, these aren't caves per se, but places where nature has sculpted an overhang where you can step inside and feel secluded

- bluffs, peninsulas, promontories, and islands; natural and magical energies seem concentrated in such places

- places with a natural view, especially sites which offer a good view of the rising of the Sun and Moon

- early religious sites and pioneer cemeteries, these were often sited according to an intuitive sense of propriety

- the grounds of historical sites and monuments

- quarries, oil fields, drainage ditches and canals, and railroad right-of-ways, although these are scars that humans have inflicted on Mother Earth, they do afford sanctuary to a variety of animals; in areas saturated with malls and condos, they provide a veritable oasis

In seeking out these sites, you'll come to find that there are places that inspire you, give you a sense of solitude and sanctuary, places that recharge you, even places that can absorb any negative energies you may be carrying around.[8] However, as pointed out before, you don't always need to have a practical purpose for going to a power spot, sometimes the purpose is just to be there. In addition to gaining energy from such places, you can also help to reenergize your own locale.

Exchanging Good Energy with Nature

A number of conscientious individuals are exploring ways to give energy back to Nature. This can be described as reenchanting the landscape, and is based on the recognition that the first step in saving the environment is spiritual. This concern is expressed by Sun Bear, a Chippewa-Ojibwa medicine man and teacher, who says:

> Many parts of the sacred Earth are hungry right now. They need people to go to them and feed them with prayers and thanksgiving, with tobacco and cornmeal. When enough people do this, many parts of the Earth will come alive.[9]

Frederick McLaren Adams, founder of a group called Feraferia, which means "Nature Celebration" or "Festival," has spent over four decades teaching Earth-based spirituality. Among the many projects that Adams has initiated and worked on has been the re-creation of a geomantic corridor running from Punta Banda near Ensenada to Point Lobos south of Carmel, California. It links into some Chumash Indian sites, including the isthmus of Santa Catalina, and its purpose is to send blessings all along the way, for the healing of the coast. In a conversation of March 8, 1992, he discussed reciprocity and spiritual confluence with the Earth, emphasizing the importance of "being in her, asking for nothing, trying to give, and telling her you simply want to serve. When you take that approach, all good things will flow from that."[10] Adams believes that we need to court and caress the spirits of Nature again, because we've treated them so horrendously.

Toward this end, one technique which Adams has been prac-ticing since the fifties involves "caressing" the landscape. To do this, you stand at a good vantage point in an appropriate outdoor area, and you lovingly trace the outline of the landscape with your hands. Adams likes to work with mountains this way, but it can also be done with trees, lakes, etc. By the fifth pass, or whenever you feel you're really in attunement with the spirit of that land-scape, you can pull the energy in toward yourself, wrap it around your body, then push it back with your healing and blessings.

It's always important to humbly ask permission of a place to do such things. It doesn't matter whether the place in question is an ancient power site or just a pleasant local nature spot. To do this, you extend your intuition in order to find out whether your inter-actions are welcome. In the example of caressing the landscape, you would tell the Spirit of Place that your intent is to take the energy out long enough to commingle it and amplify it, then give it back. The purpose is to empower it as a sacred place and "return the human soul to Earth." If you feel a negative response, then simply don't go through with your intentions. Adams points out:

There will be signs of cooperation if you enter a place that it is amenable to your intentions. Animals will always appear in a dramatic sort of way, and you get that special tingle, you know that the place is happy that you're coming back to do this.

Fred Adams also feels that regular spiritual work is important, and there are a number of things he does on a daily basis. At 8 P.M. each evening he says a prayer for the protection of the rain forest,[11] and then at 9 P.M. he honors Gaia Chthon, using James Hillman's term for the more ancient, pre-Greek name which refers to the imagination of the Earth, the soul of the Earth (as opposed to just the body of the Earth), or the anima mundi. He shares the technique for this spiritual practice.

Gaia Chthon

At 9 P.M., light a candle as you face north, and say:

Gaia Chthon,
Let those of us who would serve you,
All meet in or through the living core of the Earth,
*   your beating heart,*
*   whither this flame flees.*

At this point, blow out the flame and imagine that you are following it down into the center of the Earth, whose core could be pictured as a glowing white star. Then say:

Here at the center of the Earth,
In the white star womb,
Let us reweave the web of sacred places,
*   among the folds of Earth's skyward flesh,*
And preserve the raiment of Gaia,
*   in which she emerged from the last ice age.*
That precious viridian raiment,
*   wherein she gave us birth, nurtured us,*
*   and taught us all the ways of love.*
Now let us return that love to her
*   and share it with all her children*
And from this time forward serve her well,
*   making relations with all beings.*

Now, imagine that you are watching the flame, that you see it again, there in the center of the Earth, and follow it back upwards to the surface, until you are home again, back in your body. You can then relight the candle if you wish to let it burn for a while, and say,"Ho! So be it."

If you don't feel comfortable with visualization, the Gaia Chthon invocation would still be suitable as a silent prayer.

Fred Adams originally started this practice some time ago, by asking all of his friends to light a candle for the Earth at 9 P.M. each evening, and then to offer whatever personal prayers or devotions they could.[12] He has been surprised to find that the practice has caught on, spread across the country, and is being performed by people he doesn't even know. When we discussed this, I pointed out that all the people who share this practice can be considered to be part of a "consodality," members of a special society working to heal the Earth. Setting 9 P.M. aside for this purpose brings the energies of many people into synchronization. Fred says that 9 P.M. is the hour of the Earth; you can perform the Gaia Chthon at 9 P.M. in your local time zone. Doing the Gaia Chthon at this time enables you to be synchronized with others in your time zone. If 9 P.M. isn't convenient for you, it's fine to perform the Gaia Chthon whenever you can.

Living with Nature's Rhythms

In concluding this chapter, I want to emphasize that one way to attune to Nature's playful energies is to bring yourself more in harmony with the rhythms of the living Earth. This is done by integrating more natural activities into your life style, observing the subtle changes brought by the progression of the seasons, as well as day and night, and in all ways achieving a comfortable familiarity with Nature's ways.

Endnotes

1. Brown's works include: *The Tracker, The Search, Tom Brown's Field Guide to Wilderness Survival, Tom Brown's Field Guide to Nature Observation and Tracking, Tom Brown's Field Guide to City and Suburban Survival, Tom Brown's Field Guide to Living with the Earth, Tom Brown's Guide to Wild Edible and Medicinal Plants, Tom Brown's Field Guide to Nature and Survival for Children, The Vision,* and *The Quest.*

2. Brown, Tom. *The Vision.* New York: Berkley Books, 1988. Page 35.

3. Brown, Tom. *Tom Brown's Field Guide to Nature Observation and Tracking.* New York: Berkley Books, 1983. Pages 39–40.

4. Skinner, Charles M. *Myths and Legends of Flowers, Trees, Fruits, and Plants.* Philadelphia: Lippincott, 1911. Page 62.

5. Lawlor, Robert. *Voices of the First Day: Awakening in the Aboriginal Dreamtime.* Rochester: Inner Traditions, 1991. Page 40.

6. Some books that will give you a good overview of Nature's magical places include: *Sacred Places, How the Living Earth Seeks Our Friendship* by James A. Swan, (Santa Fe: Bear and Co., 1990); *The Power of Place, Sacred Ground in Natural and Human Environments* by James A. Swan, (Wheaton: Theosophical Publishing House, 1991); *The Earth Spirit, Its Ways, Shrines and Mysteries* by John Michell, (New York: Thames and Hudson, 1975); and *Power Trips, Journeys to Sacred Sites as a Way of Transformation* by Cynthia L. Corbett, Ph.D. (Santa Fe: Timewindow Publications, 1988).

7. It's long been noticed that places where we can connect with the Earth Spirit have therapeutic qualities, and people often are attracted to these places to recharge and relax, even to be healed. Ambience isn't the only reason why such places are special. Being near water or walking among trees and plants really does make us feel better because we experience an atmosphere charged with negative ions, which have genuine refreshing and soothing affects on people. Some writers suggest that *prana* or *ki* is intensified by having a lot of negative ions in the air combined with a favorable electromagnetic field.

8. When you locate a place that absorbs negativity, you may find that you can direct it into the ground, a rock, or tree—a place that can

absorb it without being harmed itself. In such places, the Earth can "eat" negativity, digest it, and transform it for the good of the living.

9. Sun Bear. *Honoring Sacred Places.* from Lehrman, Frederic, ed., *The Sacred Landscape.* Berkely, CA: Celestial Arts, 1988.

10. From a personal conversation with Frederick McLaren Adams, March 8, 1992.

11. Fred credits his former wife, Svetlana Butyrin, for this suggestion.

12. Fred encouraged this practice partially in honor of the memory of Jim Ordonez, a friend who had been instrumental in the recreation of geomantic corridors, and had made orgone accumulators and placed them in fountainhead places, where the healing energy of the Earth rises to meet that of the sky.

Chapter 8

Good Things Coming In

The "Good Things Coming In" spell is a special magical operation that covers a lot of bases. It is to be performed over the space of a month, a Moon Cycle, or any other convenient specified period of time. This spell's purpose is to open channels of abundance and opportunity. It encompasses luck, money, and prosperity, but love, friendship, and other intangible things can be invited in as a result.

This spell should be fun to do, and carried out in a light-hearted manner. It's in keeping with the philosophy of playful magic because it doesn't call for you to worry or focus on all of the things you haven't got, but it does provide a pleasant way to attract a lot of good stuff into your life. In the course of drawing many good things in to you, you might even find some of the items on your back burner list showing up.

Welcoming Luck

It doesn't matter when you begin this magical working, although the most favorable day is the first day of the Waxing Moon, (i.e. after the New Moon). It's also nice to choose auspicious days such as the first day of a week, month, or year, or a special holiday. (Note: It's easier to carry this magical program out when the weather is fair, not in the middle of your rainy season or winter.)

This spell doesn't require a lot of psychic effort, but to get it launched, you will need to do a bit of housework. First, you must sweep and groom your front walkway (if you live in a house). Then, wash your doors, lintels, thresholds, windowsills, telephones, and mailbox. Polish any brass fixtures on your door or mailbox; polished objects reflect light better, which gives them a more magical quality. If you're really pressed for time, or this is a particularly big job for you, you can carry this out over a series of days. When you are ready to start the cleanup, say:

This is an invitation to abundance.
I'm making good luck welcome,
That all good things may enter here.

As you engage in this cleanup, mentally repeat such affirmations as, "All good things now enter here," from time to time.

Next, get some scented oil, and go over the above mentioned objects again, rubbing the oil into them with a clean, new cloth.

You may be able to find essential oils at import stores, florists, candle shops, and craft stores that carry supplies for making potpourris and candles, and interesting blends can also be found at occult and New Age stores. You may have to go out of your way to get the oil, but going outside your normal boundaries will add power to the spell. Any pleasing scent will be suitable, but some traditional fragrances for attracting luck and prosperity include bergamot, clove, ginger, marjoram, mint, and vetivert. It's best if you can find natural oils, not synthetic oils, although natural oils are higher priced. Occult shops will often carry specially mixed products with suggestive titles such as, *Fast Luck, Lady Luck, Come Inside,* and *Money Drawing.* Other good luck blends whose names are less explanatory, include *Black Cat* and *Seven Powers.*

Since essential oils tend to be expensive, you can stretch them for the purposes of this spell by mixing a few drops of the essential oils with natural base oils. Regular cooking oils such as coconut, safflower, or sunflower, can be used. If you can find jojoba oil, this is ideal because it keeps longer, being a natural liquid wax rather than a true oil. For anointing wooden objects, you could also mix a few drops of the essential oil with rubbing oil for wood products.

There are two precautions to bear in mind when working with oils as suggested:

1. Be careful about letting undiluted essential oils touch your skin—some of them can cause minor irritation.

2. Some oils and oil combinations may leave a sticky residue or grease spots on some types of surfaces, rather than being absorbed. To determine whether you have this problem, do a patch test by dabbing a small amount of the oil blend on a small, out-of-the-way section of the surface. If it makes the surface sticky, modify this magical working by dabbing only a few small dots of the oil on selected areas, or by only putting the oil on surfaces that can take it.

While you are rubbing or dabbing the oil blend on the door frames and other items, repeat to yourself, "Good things are coming in. Lucky things, beautiful things, bright things. Many things through many channels," or any other affirmations you feel are appropriate. By just calling for "good things," you are being very nonspecific. For this reason, this spell can attract a larger spectrum of things that are good for you: money, material necessities and various luxuries, good news, information, job offers, helping hands, calls and visits from friends, and so on.

Once you have completed all of the cleaning, polishing and anointing, anoint a scented candle with the same oil. (See *Appendix I* for anointing and use of candles.) Then, light the candle and hold your hands above it in an attitude of blessing, saying:

The spell is now begun,
All good things now come to me,
All good luck is welcomed here.

Allow the candle to burn for a while, adding to the pleasant scent of your home.

Priming the Pump

The next phase of the spell involves priming the pump. As mentioned in Chapter 3, setting yourself up for success in this way is a positive affirmation, a magical act that opens channels of energy. To prime the pump for the Good Things Coming In spell, you simply see to it that something good—at least something you consider to be good—is brought back into your home each day for a month.

To kick off the first day of your Good Things Coming In spell, you might want to purchase or obtain something very special as the first good luck item to be brought in. As you return with the item, approaching the threshold of your house, you can hold the item up in salutation, saying, "I'm bringing luck into my house."

Some days you'll find good things naturally coming in through your mail, good news coming in over the phone, friends coming in for a visit, or just in doing your regular necessary shopping you'll be bringing good things back in with you. However, on days when nothing comes in or is expected to come in, you'll be required to go out and find something and bring it in for yourself or other members of your household. Every time something good comes or is brought into your home, whether it is something that you planned or something unexpected, say a simple thank-you such as, "I give thanks for this token of my good fortune," or an affirmation such as, "Everything good comes to me."

Luck-Bringing
Colors

Consider color when bringing material objects into your home, whether they are items you buy, or found items such as bird feathers, flowers, beads, marbles, smooth beach glass, (a.k.a. "salt glass" or "mermaids' tears"), and ribbons. The following colors have their own magic, inviting different types of luck:

BLACK . . . . speaks of deep mysteries

BLUE . . . . a promise of peace & contentment

BROWN . . . . security for hearth and home

GOLD . . . . many kinds of riches

GREEN . . . . abundance, growth and healing

ORANGE . . . . personal pride and enthusiasm

PINK . . . . friendship and comfort

PURPLE . . . . you can expect something unique

RED . . . . love enters your life

SILVER . . . . mysterious and romantic adventures

WHITE . . . . purity and quality of experience

YELLOW . . . . look forward to happiness

For a more extensive explanation on the symbolism of color, see Appendix II.

There are a lot of simple ways that you can get the ball rolling on this. As previously mentioned, by bringing in your regular groceries you are already bringing good stuff in. Be consciously aware of this fact as you do your shopping. You can make things more interesting by buying a few special delicacies, or by going out of your way to shop in some more interesting or exotic places. Fun food items are especially good to bring home, since you need to eat anyway. At least when you're bringing food in, you're not piling up a lot of dust catchers. You might also want to spread your normal shopping out a bit, so you can be more assured of having something to bring in each day.

You can also go out and treat yourself or family members to some special things—things you've been putting off or that you normally would be reluctant to buy—in order to give this spell a boost. Of course, you have to be practical about what your own financial limitations are and take care not to overspend. There is no need to put yourself at risk, since there are also things you can do for this spell that involve no expense.

If your personal financial resources don't allow you to go shopping often, you can always bring in found objects. A penny found in the street is an omen of good fortune. (Remember to bless the penny and say a little thank-you to your deity or to the Living Universe when you pick it up.) You can also bring in things like shiny pebbles, sea shells, wild flowers picked by the roadside, colorful autumn leaves that you could make into a centerpiece, and other sorts of treasures from nature. Found objects that you bring in can have their own magical meanings. (See *Luck-Bringing Colors* and *Symbolism of Found Objects* in this chapter.)

Another way to have lots of good things to bring home with no expense is to make frequent runs to the library. Personally, whenever I'm in the library loading my arms with books, I feel like I've won one of those contests where the winners get to run up and down the aisles of a store, filling a shopping cart with as many goodies as they can manage.

Sending and receiving things through the mail is another valid way to open channels of good for the purpose of this spell. One way to do this is to order goodies through mail-order catalogs. This serves as an affirmation that good things are coming to you, there in your home. You have no way of knowing which particular day your goods will arrive, but at least you'll have the expectation that things will be arriving in the near future. As with shopping, you have to be wise about not ordering more than you can comfortably afford or that you don't really need.

Some companies have mail-in rebates that offer refunds on certain products or at least high value coupons. Many consumers don't bother with them because it's hard to keep track of all the rules, receipts, and proofs-of-purchase they require. However, if you have time on your hands, this is another option that will prime the pump by bringing money in through the mail.

Another way of using the mail that is worth the expense is sending greetings to your friends and relatives. In today's busy world, we do not do enough of this anyway. At least some of the people you write to will be prompted to write back, and just a friendly greeting coming to you through the mail is an affirmation of good coming in. (This can also have more far reaching consequences; many opportunities come through our "connections." This is a pleasant way to keep our networks open.)

Tangible or material objects are not the only things one should think about bringing in when trying to open the channels of good. Invite friends and loved ones over more often. Bring home jokes, gentle gossip, or cartoons to share with the other members of your household. And if a refreshing breeze or cheerful sunbeam comes through your window, count it as a blessing, and give it a little welcome.

While working on the Good Things Coming In spell, bear in mind that you can help it a lot by circulating: getting around, going to lots of different places, socializing with many different persons. These actions will definitely serve to open many more potential channels of opportunity, adventure, and abundance.

If your friends are also interested in performing this spell at the same time you are, you can help each other by phoning with pleasant news, sending cartoons and jokes back and forth, inviting everyone over for tea, and so on.

Symbolism of Found Objects

The following are a few of the types of objects that can be commonly found on the streets, beaches, sidewalks, parking lots, and railroad tracks of America. Even such simple objects can serve as omens and have symbolic meanings:

ACORN . . . . good health and growth in all things

BUTTON . . . . happiness in your home

COIN . . . . prosperity

GULL FEATHER . . . . . . freedom to do what you want

JAY FEATHER . . . . opportunities

KEY . . . . you'll find something you've been seeking (an old-fashioned key is especially lucky)

PINE CONE . . . . promises for future enrichment

SEA SHELL . . . . self-betterment; can also invite the enjoyment of physical love

For a special outing, go out on a scavenger walk to see how many of these or other interesting objects you can find.

Wrapping It Up

As the month progresses, you can reinforce the Good Things Coming In spell by reapplying the scented oil to your doors, although this is not necessary. To keep track of progress, you could also make a list or daily notation on the calendar of which special thing was brought in each day.

When your month or lunar cycle is completed, you can close the spell by lighting a candle of any color that pleases you, sitting for a few moments in meditation, taking stock of your accomplishments, then thanking your Deity, acknowledging all of the blessings in your life. You can say the following closing:

This spell is complete, but never ending.
Many good things are here for me.
Many good things are coming in for me.
So it is, and so shall it ever be!

It will no longer be necessary for you to purposely bring good things in every day, as the spell will continue to go on working. Your efforts will have set the wheels in motion and caused channels of prosperity and opportunity to have opened up for you. Once the energy is flowing in that direction, it should continue to build, and each new success will reinforce it. However, you may find this enjoyable enough to want to do it at regular intervals, say seasonally or yearly. In fact, you may find simple ways to bring small things in so that it becomes a daily habit.

There's no need to worry, should you be unable to complete the month suggested for this spell, or if you have some interruptions which make it impossible for you to bring good things in on certain days. Again, the important thing is that you started the energy in motion. This is good magic, good energy, and it will continue to build, regardless of interruptions. There are no negative consequences. If you are bothered about missing a day, you could always make it up by just bringing in a little something extra the next day, and affirming that's what you're doing.

One nice thing about the Good Things Coming In spell is that it's something that you can do for a friend or loved one. You might want to send someone special something nice in the mail each day of the month or regularly bring them a series of little trifles as a special birthday present, or just to do something extra special. You can decide how much expense you want to put into it. If you're not able to afford very much, you could always just send a quick, cheerful note, and maybe a funny cartoon or news clipping each day for a week or a month. That way, your main cost would be in postage. If your loved one is a person who would be bothered by the idea of your practicing magic, you don't have to explain that this is a "magical spell." Tell him or her this is something you just felt like doing. Incidentally, sending things out also strengthens the Good Things Coming In spell because you affirm that you are a person with resources, and that you are actively taking an initiative in opening channels of abundance.

Chapter 9

Weaving Perpetual Magic into Daily Life

When we think of magical "spells," we often think of magical workings that are "once and done," elaborate ceremonies performed with a desire to bring something of special importance into one's life. However, some spells can be open-ended. These are magical operations carried out over a long period of time, even for the entirety of one's life, to affirm, attract, and reinforce things that are always desirable, like prosperity, health, happiness, and love.

Perpetual spells (and Almost Perpetual spells) incorporate actions that are done on a daily basis for a specified period of time, or every day of your life. If not done daily, they can be performed at certain regular intervals, such as certain days each week, month, or Moon cycle (such as the night of the Full Moon), or on special occasions such as holidays. The actions involved can be simple, daily chores, but they are performed with ritual consciousness—the awareness that you are turning ordinary actions into a magical rite by infusing them with positive energy directed toward a greater good. The principle here is that you are continually building and adding to what you've already started. We often feel we are locked into the routines of daily life, and we are powerless to make any changes. With these types of spells comes a sense of assurance that you are acting on your environment in a very special way, making things better, steadily and surely.

This chapter presents a collection of activities that enable you to continually weave magic into the tapestry of daily life. You'll notice that some of these spells seem to lend themselves to certain purposes. The magical suggestions that involve doing something to your home, garden, or automobile are especially appropriate for protection, prosperity, and security, while tending to personal grooming or fitness with a sense of ritual consciousness is perfect for enhancing health and beauty, attracting love, and building personal power. However, most of these activities are such that you can name any magical goal or purpose you choose. For example, if you are concerned about overall protection for yourself and your family, you can do one of the add-on crafts, such as the charm quilt, the garland, or the macrame, with the intention that every time you add a square, a bead, or a knot, you are sending additional psychic energy to build a circle of protection around your loved ones.

There are extra uses for the activities in this chapter. If you are in the practice of saying daily affirmations, you can add to some of these projects or carry out some of these activities while reciting your affirmations. (See *Appendix IV* on affirmations.) You can combine these actions with saying thank-you for various blessings you've received, as a way of commemorating those blessings. Just knowing that you're working on a perpetual spell can put you in a magical mood or help get you psyched up for certain objectives.

In addition to building and reinforcing desired qualities, a Perpetual spell is a symbolic act. It makes the affirmation that magic is ever-present in your life, and that you are strong in your own power, continually bringing new magic into your world.

Getting Started: Turning Simple Actions into Spells

If you would like to launch one of these ongoing magical spells, just look over the selection which follows, while at the same time thinking about what sort of qualities and things you want to attract into your life. Choose a project or practice that appeals to you and seems appropriate to your goals. It's OK to do several different projects with several different purposes in mind, but choosing just one special one is probably more convenient.

Decide in advance how often you will want to work on your project or activity. It can be something you do daily, or it can be done weekly, monthly, on the night of the Full Moon, certain holidays, or once a year (if it's major or expensive). With some of the activities, you might consider whether you want to discontinue them after a certain time period. You pick the timing and occasion to match the nature of the project and its magical purpose.

When you have assembled your materials and are ready to start, think about your magical objective and your reason for choosing this particular project or activity, then visualize yourself working on it for however long it takes, depending on whether it's the sort of project that will be completed at some point or an ongoing activity. Now, say out loud:

> *I here initiate a work of magic.*
> *With every step I take,*
> (Here you could say something specific like, *"With every bead I add..."* or *"With every candle I light..."*)
> *I send lasting power to my objective, which is...*
> (Briefly describe your purpose.)
> *As I begin this enchantment,*
> *so is the magic set in motion.*

As you begin your project or practice, and each time you add to it or go back to it, visualize that you are raising magical energy and fixing it on your objective. With each addition or repetition, you can think or recite an affirmation such as "The power grows and builds," or "My magic is increasing and everlasting," or "I infuse my life with unending Enchantment," or any other affirmations that you think appropriate.

By carrying out your project or activity with the awareness that you're working on a magical spell, you elevate what may be an ordinary activity into a ritual act and add a mystical dimension to everyday life. By taking the attitude that you're a magic weaver, you also affirm your own power in all realms of life.

If for some reason your pattern gets interrupted, it's important to remember that missing a day or a week or any other occasion doesn't blow the spell. As with the Good Things Coming In spell in Chapter 8, the good energy you raise builds and carries and there are no negative consequences. When you miss an occasion, you just pick up where you normally would. If you feel compelled to, you can make up for a missed session by doubling the amount of time or material involved in the project or activity. Although nothing negative will come of slacking off on your magical projects, remember that "carry-through" is something that a lot of people in our society are seriously lacking. So, when you do have the determination to carry something out regularly, it will make a profound impression on your Unconscious.

If carrying out a certain project, activity, or practice becomes too inconvenient and you decide to indefinitely discontinue it, you can just quit, content with the knowledge that the power is already fixed. If you like, you can bring it to an end by ceremonially stating an affirmation such as:

I bless this work (or my actions),
   knowing that its power goes on and on.

When you complete a limited project such as a charm quilt, you can display it, then stand before it in an attitude of blessing, saying something like:

I bless this completed work,
    a work of skill, a work of magic.
This project is imbued with power:
    power of mind, and heart, and spirit.
With the completion of this project
    the magic is eternally fixed.

Visualize the project carrying out its magical purpose. If you really enjoyed working on that particular project, there's no reason why you can't start a new one just like it.

Following, in no significant order, are a few suggestions for projects, practices, and activities that can be employed as Perpetual spells. Chapter 3 suggested making lists to define your magical goals, and some of the objectives you may have listed, such as love or prosperity, can be worked into these projects. Despite the fact that the philosophy of playful magic recommends working on secondary goals that don't have any desperate emotions riding on them, it's OK if you find that you can work in items from your back burner list. Just remember to do the projects or activities because they are fun and meaningful, and maintain a carefree attitude when you do them.

Sensory Delights: Flowers, Candles, and Incense

An ongoing ritualistic practice that is also a treat to your senses is to burn a candle or a stick of incense, or set a single flower out in a bud vase on a daily or other regular basis. Working with these materials, particularly with living things like flowers and some of the natural materials used in incense, is wonderfully energizing. Because these materials get used up, there's the advantage that they generally don't catch dust and take up too much space. The disadvantage is that there is some expense involved, unless, like flowers, you grow your own. Here are some things to consider:

Flowers

If you love flowers and have your own garden, collect lots of bud vases and have a special area to display them. Add a new flower and vase each day, removing wilted ones as necessary. I think eight days is the best you can expect for roses or most other cut flowers; most do not last that long. If there's room in your fridge, you can put them in at night to make them last longer. Florists also recommend adding things like lemon-lime soda or sugar to their water to provide some nutrients. Since flowers symbolize the blossoming of all hopes, they are appropriate for any magical purpose. Flowers also exude a special quality of Life Force, so setting out vases can be a spell for health and vitality.

Incense and Potpourri

Burn a stick a day or add to your potpourri warmer for something pleasant to do. Your whole home and the things in it will gradually acquire a nice scent. Ancient peoples believed that incense and fragrance, with their Heavenward ascending smoke and scent, carry our wishes to the Deity and the Spiritual Powers. This makes them a suitable offering to attract luck from unseen sources and bring mysteries and wonders into the mundane world.

Candles

Burning a candle each day is a very traditional, as well as meaningful, magical and spiritual act. Depending on your resources and what's convenient, you can have small votives which can be allowed to burn down to nothing, or just burn a candle for an hour each evening, or add a candle each day and burn the whole accumulation of candles for one hour each evening. Do the last suggestion only if you don't mind your home looking like a religious shrine. The power of the Fire Element brings extra vitality to any spell, so candle burning can be used for any magical objective. The flame's association with warmth and desire makes it especially powerful for attracting both the physical and emotional qualities of love. People who like to work with candles for magical purposes choose special colors and dress the candles by anointing them with scented oils. (Refer to Appendix I and Appendix II for more information on the use of candles and color symbolism.)

Work as Ritual

Regular, physical work to maintain or improve your home or other belongings can be done with magical consciousness. Aside from being a way to get practical things done, this makes ordinary chores more meaningful. By pairing your magical purpose with physical motions, more energy is directed to your objective. This is because action and movement (i.e. motor activities), engage more areas of the brain, so you send more power than if you just performed a spell that used mental discipline alone. Here are a few common chores that you can turn into perpetual spells by performing them on a daily or regular basis.

Auto Maintenance

Clean and/or polish one segment of your car each day, even only a single headlight or panel at a time, to put this spell in motion. Perform small maintenance activities like checking your oil, water levels, tires, spark plugs, points, filters, and hoses on a regular basis. Clean or replace them as necessary. In Jungian dream analysis, a car can symbolize the way you get around in life, so dreaming about having your own transportation is a good sign because it shows that you have a measure of control plus the means to take you where you want to go. From a magical standpoint, this can mean that doing things to improve your car will speed you in the direction of your goals. Performing these actions with ritual consciousness can also serve as a spell to increase prosperity and/or safety.

Cleaning and Home Improvement

You can clean an area of your house or make some special improvement on it each day, week, or on some regular basis while affirming that you have security, prosperity, love, and/or domestic happiness. The types of cleaning and home improvement involved don't have to be major or extensive. It's enough if you're able to work on a small area each time, like dusting one room, or stripping, painting, or refinishing a part of an area or object. Incidentally, in the spirit of green magic, don't view dirt as something bad or nasty; it's earth after all. When we dust, clean, or polish an object, it then reflects light…giving subtle psychological and psychic benefits. That's one of the reasons there's something different and better about a room that's just been cleaned.

Gardening

Weeding and other garden chores can be done for a specified amount of time, or for a specified area of the garden each day or week. The symbolic connection between gardening and growth is obvious, so this can be done with the attitude that it's a spell to increase health and/or prosperity. While weeding, you can maintain a mental picture that you are purging your life of negativity. Bless the weeds, saying:

I send you away as I release my cares.
Mother Nature gives you rebirth in another place.

You can gradually add new plants or build up certain features of your property such as rock gardens, stone fences, borders, and the like, accompanying each new addition with a positive affirmation or magical intent. With the rock arrangements, going on special outings to collect rocks to bring back could also be a meaningful activity. (When I was in Arizona, I was impressed with the beautiful effects homeowners got by arranging different sizes and colors of rocks, in lieu of lawns, in order to conserve water.)

Networking, Circulating, and Socializing

Certain aspects of your actions and interactions can be consciously performed as a Perpetual spell. Some of your ordinary but repetitive comings and goings, exchanges with people, and involvement with the outside world can assume the nature of ritual. In the Good Things Coming In spell in Chapter 8, we already looked at this concept with respect to bringing channels of good into your home and your life. The following suggestions offer a way to extend your magical energies outward—a type of magic that is good for attracting friendship, support, and influence. With your various interactions, whether they are personal or more indirect, consciously try to send some "good vibes" toward the other person or persons.

Networking

Most people find it important to maintain contact with a large network of friends, relatives, and acquaintances for mutual support, advice, and assistance. Networking isn't avaricious social climbing or the "using" of other people; it's based on the recognition that in this large and complicated society of ours, we're all interdependent in a great number of ways. This type of reciprocity also strengthens the social fabric, which is why in so many tribal societies have worked out detailed reciprocal relationships and protocols.

As a Perpetual spell for "connectedness," you can do something to maintain your network on a regular basis—preferably daily. This can involve sending simple greetings by phone or mail, or doing other small things to keep in touch with a wide variety of people of many different ages, backgrounds, professions, and walks of life. You can also go out of your way to meet new people, especially persons with different interests or occupations than yours. This sort of activity will, incidentally, enable you to experience the Mercurial energies, as that archetype rules communication and interactions between people. Mercury also inspires the alchemy which brings the qualities and viewpoints of different individuals together in such a way that creative inspirations are generated and integrated. (When we want to bring change into our lives, it sometimes doesn't occur to us to simply tell our larger circle of acquaintances what we want. We overlook the possibility that people we already know may offer options, suggestions, and opportunities. So if there's something special that you're trying to manifest, just spread the word, and don't be shy.)

Turn networking activity into ritual by creating a sense of sacred space. If you write a letter each day, do it with magical awareness in a serene place and at a time set aside to be free from interruptions. Create atmosphere by playing beautiful background music, burning incense, and so on. You can say affirmations like, "I extend my sphere of influence, growing rich in my relationships and interactions." Visualize an expanding network in symbolic terms by picturing something like yourself at the center of an outward spreading circle of light, crystal spider web, or a living mandala.

Reaching Out

In Chapter 8, it was suggested that you send good things—even if only small things—to loved ones, and that you can bring good things to yourself by ordering things through the mail. These actions serve as affirmations that you're a person of resources and you're opening channels of abundance. As an extension of this,

and the networking concept, you can further make the affirmation that you're at the center of your own power, consciously acting on your world, by sending out some form of communication on a daily or other regular basis. In addition to calling and writing personal greetings to friends and relatives, you can enter various sweepstakes and contests (be careful to avoid ones that require you to pay any fees), make contributions to charities, and engage in some form of social activism by sending your opinions to politicians, businesses, or TV networks. Doing these things as a form of ritual would be a good way for anyone to help achieve personal empowerment, but it would be especially useful for certain disabled persons and shut-ins. For persons suffering from agoraphobia, this could be done to build some confidence (in combination with the proper therapy), as a prelude to reentering society.

Going Places

Regularly exploring new places, whether planned or done spontaneously, is another way to extend your personal power and magical influence, and to push the boundaries of your daily life. This is also a way to experience the Mercurial energies, as Mercury is the patron of travelers. In exploring new places, you can think of yourself as extending your magical fantasy kingdom or queendom, as suggested in Chapter 6. You can give your intuition and imagination free rein to project fantasies into any new places that strike your fancy.

Personal Pampering and Body Work

People differ in the amount of thought and attention they give to their physical health and appearance. Whether you are a person who is diligent about health and beauty or a person who tends to take your body for granted, the following suggestions for turning health and hygienic routines into ritual can certainly benefit you.

Grooming

We all have our normal grooming routines, but you can make yours a little more special by regularly treating your body to some new tonic, cosmetic, or beauty treatment. Experiment with new products or consult various herbals to learn how to make your own. Go for the exotic and the luxurious. You can perform your morning or evening routine within the context of sacred space by burning incense and playing beautiful music while you do it. Conscious attention to grooming puts you in harmony with the Goddess Aphrodite, whose gifts are pride and pleasure in yourself, and "being present" in your own body.

Exercise

An obvious way to make a magical commitment to health and beauty is through regular exercise. You might find it effective to do exercises designed to build up muscles during the Waxing Moon, and aerobic exercises to burn fat during the Waning Moon.

Use visualization to aid weight loss by picturing yourself burning fat as you would burn incense. Don't think of that fat as ugly flab, think of it as stored energy. It may have served a purpose at one time, but now you are ready to release it. Think of your exercise as burning that stored energy, releasing it into the atmosphere for Mother Earth to metabolize. To reinforce the visualization, burn incense first thing in the morning while mentally chanting:

Burning incense, burning fat.
Releasing energy into the air...into the earth...

As you do this, feel yourself getting pleasantly warmer and warmer as you stoke up your metabolism. Some people who are concerned with losing fat can't see the point in exercises that won't immediately result in weight loss. However, exercises designed for body building steadily increase lean muscle mass, which keeps your body metabolizing at a higher rate and burning more calories, even while you sleep. These types of exercise, including martial arts and dance, will put you in touch with Mars energy, which complements the Aphrodite qualities previously mentioned.

Handicrafts and Hobbies
You Can Build On

There are a number of leisure time activities that can be infused with magical meaning, using the same principles described throughout this chapter. More magical uses for arts, crafts, and toys will be listed in Chapters 10 and 11. However, the following projects can be turned into ongoing spells because you add to them little by little, over a long period of time.

Collectibles

People who are into collecting can tell you that it's a lifetime preoccupation, and the amount of love most collectors put into their treasures makes them animate with psychic energy. (For this, and for ecological reasons, collecting done nowadays ought to be done selectively and with forethought.)[1] To turn a collection into a Perpetual spell, you combine magical intent with each new piece you add. For pricier items you may need to be budget conscious, so just acquire them on special occasions or to commemorate special events, in order to avoid spending too much.

Collectors intuitively tend to collect knick-knacks and miniatures that represent qualities or things they would like to manifest in their lives. Dolls, doll houses, model railroads, and other toys are popular with collectors, and more about their magical uses will be discussed in Chapter 11. Collecting domestic items like thimbles, souvenir spoons, and salt and pepper shakers can be combined with a wish for peace, happiness, and protection of your home. Sticker collections are popular with kids, but there's no reason why a playful adult couldn't start one. Pins and buttons are easy to col-

lect, and serve some of the same purposes as lucky charms. Coin and stamp collecting are ever-popular, and symbolize prosperity. Collecting music, entertainment tapes, videos, or discs affirms that you are surrounded with beauty and laughter. Collecting natural objects such as rocks and shells allows you to commune with the elements and work with materials that are strong in natural magic. People intuitively collect representations of totem animals, even if they don't fully understand what a totem is.

It's fun to look through special collectors' catalogs just to see the sort of objects that are available. Many of them are imaginative and fantastical. I don't think there's any type of collecting activity that you couldn't infuse with some magical energy and meaning, but collections especially tend to be material affirmations of abundance and growth. Also, the individual collectible items may hold symbolic significance. Refer to Appendix III, to learn more about the playfully magical interpretations of some collectable objects.

Garlands

Create a garland by adding beads daily, weekly, or monthly, while stating positive affirmations or magical intent. You can make knots in the strand, or hang charms, toys, or small Christmas ornaments from it with a little bit of ceremony. Such garlands can be used as decorations framing windows, hung from ceilings, run along banisters, and so on. Using the same ideas, you can create necklaces and other beaded projects by adding one bead at a time on a regular basis until you complete the project, then start another one. You can add to a paper chain on a regular basis, making it meaningful by writing a wish or an affirmation on each link.

Charm Strings

Based on the same idea and popular at the same times as charm quilts, charm strings are made by stringing 999 buttons together on a single strand of thread. Young girls believed that when you added the 999th button to the string, your true love would appear.

Charm Quilts

Although sewing and fabric crafts are more thoroughly discussed in Chapter 10, the "Charm Quilt" is especially suitable for an ongoing spell. Traditionally, these quilts are created by using 999 different fabric squares and never repeating a fabric, with tumbler, square, rectangle, and hexagon patterns being particularly popular. In *The Fabric Lover's Scrap Book,* author Margaret Dittman points out that this craft was popular in the late 1800s, then made a resurgence during the Depression.[2] Dittman says, "The best charm quilts contain *trompe l'oeil* tricks—they fool the eye by clever juxtapositions of fabric almost identical." To get your squares to equal 999, you'll have to calculate so you can get the size quilt you want by using rows of 27 x 37 pieces, which would be fairly small units, even for a king-sized quilt. Not all charm quits used that exact number. You could use larger, but fewer squares, or you could even make a "postage stamp" quilt by using more, really minuscule squares. It was believed that the first night you sleep under a charm quilt, whatever you dream will come true.

Coloring Poster

In Chapter 3, it was suggested that as a way of saying thank-you for blessings received, you can gradually fill in the segments of one of those large coloring posters. This could also be done as an ongoing spell. Perform a little ritual where, each time you say your daily affirmations, you color in a new segment. This is a way of feeling like you're creating something tangible while you're doing your inner work or shaping your magical reality.

Macrame

By adding knots over a period of time, you can turn any macrame project into an ongoing spell. Naturally, beads and charms can be worked in. One impressive work I've seen was a wide macrame curtain (which was being created with magical intent) to divide two rooms. A good affirmation is, "I'm creating a web of magic."

Charming Accessories

The use of little metal or plastic charms is related to the significance of collectibles, but I feel it deserves its own section because charms are currently popular and abundant. (If you have children, you find they accumulate a lot of these as party favors and from gumball machines.) For the symbolic meanings of some of these popular charms, refer to Appendix III. Charms can be material affirmations of qualities or things that you want. Make the statement, "I already possess this thing, it is already so." Although the section on goals for playful magic in Chapter 3 suggested working only on the objectives on your secondary list, you can break the rules if you acquire some nice charms that signify your main goals. Just don't dwell on them, focusing on what you don't have. When you're admiring your charms, admire them all equally. Here are some ways to make use of charms and various other small mementos.

Personal Decoration

Charms are most commonly used in jewelry, hung from bracelets, wrist watches, necklaces, earrings, or grouped in a bunch and hung from a pendant. You can also attach them to belts, hats, jackets, barrettes, or even sew them onto ankle socks to attract good luck and the other qualities that the charms depict.

Tree of Life Jewel Collage

Elaborate "Tree of Life" forms created by a collage of jewels and all sorts of charms are a craft entry I've seen featured at the Los Angeles County Fair in past years. (It's always fun to try to spot all the charm symbols worked into the design.) These enchanting trees are made by gluing the jewelry and charms to a velvet-like backing. They mainly consist of broken-off pieces of costume jewelry, such as earrings and pins. The charms and other pieces used can include personal and family mementos and small items of memorabilia, like scout and fraternity pins. The trees either tend to take the triangular forms of pines or the spreading forms of oaks.

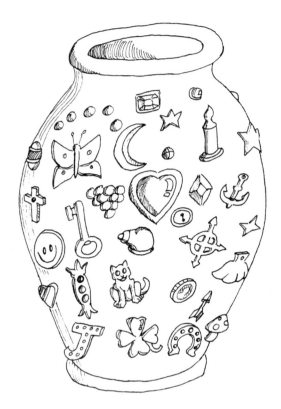

Sometimes the creator outlines the tree with braid or contrasting fabric; sometimes the jewels themselves define the outlines.

Like all projects that use charms, the symbols can be used magically to depict things you want to bring into your life. However, creating a Tree of Life really becomes a super-special magical spell when you turn it into a family tree and include photo portraits of your loved ones, set in miniature gilt or silverized frames and surrounded by all the other charms and jewels. Then, not only does it convey a magical wish for the things that are symbolized by the charms, it also makes a statement of family bonding and eternal togetherness.

I have been slowly collecting suitable charms and other items to create such a tree for my own family, but I don't expect to have enough to even begin working on it for several years. That's because I only want to use things that have sentimental meaning; I want to avoid using lots of filler items. My magical intent is family continuity, togetherness, happiness, and blessings.

Memory Jars

Earlier in this century, young people enjoyed creating "memory jars." This was done by covering a common vase with clay, and then sticking charms, costume jewels, small toys, and other mementos into it. If you want to use this as an ongoing magical activity, you can use the same principles as in the Tree of Life. (If you want to use air-hardening clay, you may have to first collect all the charms and objects before you actually prepare the vase.)

Miscellaneous

Charms can be added to garlands and macrame projects as described in *Handicrafts.* You can also stick charms into candles

with the idea that, as they burn down, power will be sent off to attract those things into your life. It's also fun to use stickers as charms, sending them through the mail to convey good wishes.

Other Magical Actions

Witch's Bottle

Traditionally, a "witch's bottle" is a bottle or jar that you fill with unpleasant things like nails, needles, and broken glass, then bury under your threshold as a protective spell to deflect any evil or negativity coming your way. There's another kind of witch's bottle where you add snipped threads from your sewing projects to a jar one at a time, then set the jar in the rafters for protection of your house. You can use this idea to make a charm to attract good things to you, and make it an ongoing spell by putting nice things in it, one at a time.

You can fill a bottle with found items like pennies, marbles, sea shells, salt glass, and buttons, or you can create a witch's bottle filled with nothing but colorful plastic charms. You can keep it by the door or any other special place until it's filled. Then you can continue to display it, hide it in your attic, or bury it as is done with some of the traditional witch's bottles. The advantage of using found items is that it can be an affirmation that pleasant surprises are always coming your way. You can also gradually fill jars with things like different potpourri ingredients and spices, with the intent of welcoming good fortune.

Wishes and Votives

Having a routine for making wishes or leaving offerings to honor the spirits of place is always pleasant, and can be done with the attitude that you're working toward a special goal or just adding to a magical "energy bank." Regularly throwing coins in a wish-

ing well is an obvious way to do this, and it's nice to know that they usually go toward worthwhile charities.

If you own property, tying ribbons on your trees is another traditional form of wishing, as well as making offerings to the fairies. Other votives include incense, candles, flowers, wreaths, libations, and the sprinkling of grain or cornmeal.

Curiosity

Last but not least, doing something that will engage your curiosity on a regular basis is a very magical activity, and knowledge is something you can always add to. Consider going on an unending Information Quest. Things to pique your curiosity can be found in any field of knowledge, the exploration of nature, all the arts, family history and genealogy, psychological approaches to understanding people, healing therapies, and an infinite number of other possibilities. Have a plan for regularly accessing libraries and other media for the knowledge you want, also make a point of talking to lots of people, including older and younger people, strangers, and persons whose job it is to offer information, such as museum guides, rangers, or librarians. Don't neglect to exercise your curiosity through emotional forms of expression, hands-on activities, and other physical actions and non-linear types of learning.

Endnotes

1. In discussing collections, I am not recommending the type of mindless acquisition that is such a problem in our society. I believe less is better. If you aren't already collecting stuff, it's preferable not to start. However, knowing human nature, as well as the nature of our consumer society, I realize that acquisition is inevitable. Collecting fewer things, but ones that are of higher quality and richer in personal meaning, is one way to waste fewer resources.

2. Dittman, Margaret. *The Fabric Lover's Scrap Book*. Radnor: Chilton, 1988.

Chapter 10

Artful Activities with Magical Meaning

We all know arts and crafts are fun as well as therapeutic, but they can be put to interesting magical uses as well.

In Chapter 9, some of the suggestions for weaving magic into daily life showed how to unite certain craft projects with magical purposes. You can also use the artistic medium to create visual images and tangible representations of the things you desire. Such a work of art or craftsmanship is the material equivalent of a positive affirmation because the thing you want is portrayed as already existing. Anything you can do with your hands also affirms the magical philosophy that you are the Creator of your own reality. Designing, drawing, weaving, building, shaping, molding, patterning—they all reinforce this concept. As you work on a piece of art or a craft project, you can consciously imprint every action—every stitch or brush stroke—with magical intent and psychic energy by saying a suitable affirmation or just by thinking about the special goal you have in mind.

The how-tos in this chapter incorporate magical techniques, using arts and crafts as spells. These projects require actions—gathering and manipulating materials, making things with your hands—as well as visualizing, planning, and carrying out designs. Whenever you do something with your hands or go through some other kind of physical action, it engages more areas of your brain than if you were just thinking about it or visualizing it. In magical practice, this adds extra power to your operation. In spiritual philosophy, this engages more facets of your being.

Your projects will likely involve a variety of colors and designs, which can have their own symbolic meanings. For more information on the magical symbolism of color and design, refer to Appendix II and Appendix III.

Any art or craft project you complete with all of these things in mind has a triple meaning, being a work of magic, art, and love. This is even more meaningful when the item is made as a gift for a loved one. If the finished product is something that gets daily use, such as a quilt or an item of clothing, that use, combined with the knowledge of its special purpose, reinforces both the love and the magic.

Starting and Finishing

When you work on a craft project that has some magical intent, you may not feel a need to do anything "ritualistic" to start it or complete it because you may feel that getting the idea to do something and then gathering the materials initiates the magic, and that admiring the completed product binds it, that is to say "fixes" the magic in place. However, it can be very helpful to have affirmations and visualizations to help you focus on your magical objective. For the various projects listed in this chapter, whether they involve drawing, painting, sewing, pasting, or whatever, you can do the following rite to formally begin the magical spell.

When you are ready to begin your project, lay out all of your materials and stand before them. Handle them while visualizing the creative process you will be going through. Picture yourself working on the project for however long it takes. Think of the magical qualities or goals you want the project to achieve or be imbued with. Picture the finished project, and visualize your magical goals being brought into reality. Now, hold your hands over your materials in a gesture of blessing and say:

I am Creator and Inventor and Shaper.
My designs are templates for reality,
*   and reality is shaped in my imagining.*
All my patterns are imbued with power.
All my creations are made with heart.
As I begin this project,
*   so does the magic go forth.*

You can alter the above affirmation, tailoring it to the type of art, craft, or project you will be doing, by saying things like "I am the weaver of magical webs," or "I paint the canvass of reality."

As you proceed with your project and go through the various motions, visualize directing magical energy into the materials and into the product, pulling Cosmic force and Earth energy into your body and through your hands. Visualize this energy speeding your desires into reality. (You don't have to make these visualizations every single moment. If you remember to do it from time to time, that's quite OK.) If you like, you can occasionally think or voice an affirmation such as, "I'm weaving the threads of magic," "I'm the master/mistress of magical artistry," "I'm the maker of tangible magic," or any other affirmations you think appropriate.

When you have completed the project, prop it up or display it, then stand in front of it and say something like:

> *Now I celebrate the completion*
> *of this work of magic artistry.*
> *This project is animate with power—*
> *power of mind, and heart, and spirit.*
> *With the completion of this project*
> *comes the fulfillment of my desires.*

Once again, visualize the magical objective becoming real, just as your project has been brought into full expression.

Following, in no particular order, are some techniques you can try. These are projects enabling you to use your hands to infuse magic into substance and bring some of your desires into being. Chapter 3 suggested making lists to help you define your magical goals. Many of those objectives can be worked into projects such as the Wish Collage, mandalas, quilts, etc. Despite the fact that I recommended concentrating on secondary, less important goals for the purposes of playful magic, if you find you can work in some of the items from your back burner list, that's OK. Just remember to do the projects because they are fun, and maintain a playful and carefree attitude when you work on them.

Wish Collage

An easy and enjoyable way to create a visual and tangible image of your desires is to put together a Wish Collage. To do this, simply obtain a piece of cardboard or buy a large poster board. (Artists' supply and craft stores carry poster boards in a variety of colors, but you can usually find them in the stationery and crafts sections of a lot of dime stores.) Then, you collect pictures of the things you want, cutting them out of magazines, catalogs, greeting cards, and various other sources. You make a collage with these images by arranging them in artful patterns or simply by gluing them down in a random manner on the poster board.

You can have a single collage used to picture anything you can imagine (at least anything you can find pictures of), or you can create collages with different themes or categories. For example, you could create a collage with pictures suggesting the theme "quality of life," showing people having celebrations, engaged in sports and leisure activities, having intimate relationships, enjoying quality times with their families, and so on. Then, you could also have a collage with the specific material items you desire, with pictures taken straight from advertisements and catalogs. Another collage could have fantasy images, such as castles, tropical paradises, etc.

In some cases, particularly with certain themes, you may find that it won't be possible to fill your whole poster board right away; there may be a lot of blank and open spaces. That's OK, don't feel that you're under an obligation to fill all the white space. Just let the collage develop as it will.

Space may have to be left open while you look for just the right picture to paste into that special place. Sometimes you'll find an image of something that you hadn't previously considered, and you'll feel so drawn to it that you just know you have to include it in your collage. Sometimes you'll recognize that there's an important element you want to add, but either can't pinpoint it in your mind or can't find the image you want. Keep on the lookout; you'll intuitively recognize it when you've found the picture meant to fill one of those open spaces. If you've been searching for a while for a picture to symbolize that certain something, sometimes finding it serves as a magical affirmation in and of itself. You feel a sense of triumph, and pasting it down becomes a ritual act.

While you're working on your Wish Collage and after it's finished—should you ever consider it to be finished—you can store it wherever or however you want. You can display it on the wall or hide it in a closet. You might find that there are always new things you want to add, but if at some time you should come to feel it's complete, you can either frame it or throw it away. If the collage has become rather dirty and tatty over the years so you don't want to keep it, destroying it or throwing it away won't alter the good magic you've put in motion. On the other hand, if there's something in the collage that you've changed your mind about and don't want, you can either pull it off or cover it over with the affirmation, "I release this thing, as it is no longer meaningful to me." If it should happen that you come to deem most of the content of the collage regrettable or irrelevant, you can destroy or throw away the entire project, using the same affirmation.

I have my own Wish Collage that I've been working on for years. In my case, it has lots of pictures of the beauty of country living in a four seasons climate. I was sure to include a photo of my kids in it, since I want them to be a part of everything good. As for finding pictures, I got off to a good start, but since then, only occasionally do I find something I feel like adding. I haven't filled all the spaces—partially because I haven't always been able to find pictures that really speak to me, and partially because I haven't fully defined everything I want to have in it. Despite the fact that this collage has been sitting around so long in a state of incompletion, a lot of the things in it have already materialized or been realized, including some small, incidental things that were part of larger pictures I pasted down, more for their overall symbolism or ambience.

Drawing and Painting

Whether you have experience with drawing and painting, or whether you just like to doodle, you can use your talent to accomplish the same things that are expressed in the Wish Collage, using pen or paintbrush to depict either material items you would like to

have, or qualities you would like to bring into your life. Your picture could consist of a single scene that captures the essence of what you hope to achieve, or it could be a montage of images, similar to the Wish Collage. You could also arrange your picture as a mandala.

Mandalas

A particularly meaningful way to commit desired images to paper is by creating mandalas. The word "mandala" simply means "circle." It commonly refers to a basically circular design that contains within it many smaller geometric and nongeometric designs, symbols, and patterns. These designs are concentrically arranged around a central figure, and patterned to create a sense of balance. The choice of colors used in mandalas is also laden with symbolism. (Refer to Appendix II and Appendix III for some basic symbolic meanings of the colors and geometric designs.)

Joseph Campbell, who has inspired so many people to find meaning in myth, noted that the mandala as a religious symbol and art form emerged once people started living together in large, organized groups, which caused them to want to affirm their own identity and place in the scheme of things. Mandalas are not found in the artwork of the ancient hunting and gathering people, who lived in loose-knit, free-roaming bands, and were accustomed and psychologically oriented to a certain level of independence.[1] He suggested that mandalas are microcosm/macrocosm symbols which show the individual's place within the family, within the clan, within the local society, within the human community, within the natural world, within the cosmos. The circular arrangement serves as a unifying element, and the balance of forms contributes to show the individual's relatedness and participation in the greater whole of a well-organized and balanced universe. The mandala, thus, has the psychological benefit of reconciling the struggle between the need to keep one's individuality and the need to fit into society.

Taking Campbell's interpretation into consideration, mandala making can be effective as a magical operation to help you define what you want in relationship to the rest of the world, find your niche, surround yourself with the qualities and things you love, and achieve relatedness and wholeness. It acts as both a protective and attractive talisman, depicting your place in a web of magical energies, binding outer and inner worlds. You may particularly want to try this if your are feeling a sense of frustration about not being in your "right place" in life, whether that is in regards to career, love life and relationships, environment, or all of the above. This would also be a good thing to do if you are suffering from the rundown health, nervous conditions, and low stamina that can result from being in a place that is bad for you.

To prepare small mandalas, make circles with a compass on ordinary white paper or use saucers to trace the circles, and then cut them out. Paper plates can also be used for this purpose. To make a larger mandala to encompass more pictures and symbols, get a large piece of poster board and trim the edges to make it round. Now, draw images that depict or symbolize of things or qualities you would like to manifest. If a particular object is too hard for you to illustrate, just put down a color or symbol that you feel captures some of the essence of that image. It's also OK to put down any key words that you feel summarize qualities or desires, printing or writing the words colorfully and artistically. (If you don't want to draw a mandala, you can make artful geometric arrangements with various natural materials, such as shells, stones, pine cones, seeds, etc.)

To make the project more interesting, I suggest applying the following restriction: illustrate the mandala only with crayons or wide-tipped felt markers—no pens, pencils, and fine-tipped felt markers. The finer-tipped drawing tools sometimes tend to cause us to get hung up on precision of form. Using blunter tools, such as crayons, forces us to give up precision and accuracy, enabling a freer flow of creative and emotional expression.

It doesn't matter whether you draw the images of your desires in a particular order or pattern: it's OK to put them down in random order and see what kind of patterns emerge. If you like, you can divide the circle up and assign different images to different sectors. Since mandalas tend to focus on a center which usually symbolizes the individual, or Self, you'll probably want to put a personal image or symbol in the middle.

As you arrange the various designs to form your mandala, you may find that ideas start coming to you on how to rearrange the various components of your life to put you in a better place. You may also start encountering little synchronicities that bring new elements into your personal situation and experience.

It's not necessary to keep your mandalas or do anything special with them. However, when you've accumulated enough of them, you may enjoy taping them to the wall in chronological order or in other patterns. You may find yourself referring back to them, finding meaningful patterns emerging over time, and drawing creative inspiration from them. Although the mandalas suggested here are designed to manifest things you want to bring into being, a side benefit is that contemplating your finished products will give you new insights about yourself, and you'll probably gain new perspectives each time you look at them.

If you're interested in additional techniques and applications for mandalas, Amber Wolfe presents a number of different exercises for meditation, magic, and divination that use the mandala principle in her book, *In the Shadow of the Shaman.*[2] In the section *Sacred Spells,* Wolfe suggests creating a giant mandala by sitting in the center of a white sheet or table cloth, then drawing on the cloth with permanent color marking pens, surrounding yourself with images inspired by the four directions. She says the cloth can then be used to cover yourself when you want to be comforted by its healing, energizing, or protective powers.

Maps and Floor Plans

Your magical illustrations don't have to be limited to pictures and artistic designs; diagrams such as maps, floor plans, and even charts and graphs can be drawn with magical intent.

If you regularly construct flow charts, pie charts, bar graphs, and other types of diagrams for business presentations, you may feel comfortable doing the same thing for magical purposes. Try drawing a variety of charts with designated areas representing things you would like to have—such as health, wealth, and happiness—and depict them as already thriving and increasing. Then, post them on your bulletin board where you can regularly see them. If you enjoy working with graphics programs, this is one way you can use your computer in the service of magic.

Drawing floor plans and garden diagrams is a way to help you visualize your dream house, as well as improvements you'd like to make or new things you'd like to bring into your current home.

This is a practical thing to do because it gets you focused on a course of action, but it also has psychic implications; the act of visualization makes imprints on the Ethereal Plane. (Drawing floor plans for these purposes is similar to doll house magic. See Chapter 11 for more information.)

If finding a good place to relocate to and settle down is a concern for you, particularly if you haven't already identified the best location, try drawing a map of an idealized community or type of area that you would like to live in. This is a magical action to help steer you in the direction of your dreams. It will also help you clarify what features and amenities you're looking for.

I've noticed that young people like to make maps of imaginary countries, and I tend to think such charts are a projection of their dreams and ideals. If you are a visionary person, you can draw maps of imaginary worlds which embody ideals you would like to see expressed more often in our own world, such as fertile and prosperous lands, pristine wildernesses, and cities founded with a commitment to peace and equality. For such a map, it's important to put in the descriptive titles, such as *Ancient Oak Grove, Healing Fountain, Tower of Knowledge,* and a map legend to explain special symbols. Again, by creating templates of this sort, you imprint the Ethereal Plane with your visualized images. Who's to say that such a scheme will not, in some small way, affect conditions on this plane?

When you dream at night, do you sometimes dream of special places that arouse good emotions and have sentimental meanings for you, even though they aren't part of your real life landscape? You could draw a generalized outline map of an imaginary area, then draw in these dreamscapes, using your intuition to show where to place them. The magical intent of such a map is to strengthen those emotional qualities in your waking life, and to put you into greater affinity with the world of your unconscious mind, gaining greater creativity and insight.

Modeling and Sculpting

We can make the images of our desires three-dimensional by using the same principle used in creating collages, drawings, paintings, and mandalas. Modeling with clay, salt dough, or other sculpting or casting media is a way to make representations of things you want to bring into your life. This probably works best for depicting material items, though you could make little figurines that embody qualities or emotions such as joy, celebration, or love. Miniature dioramas of indoor or outdoor scenes can also be created to portray certain ideals, similar to the use of maps and floor plans, or doll houses and model railroads. (See Chapter 11.) Such projects are very tangible. Whenever you look at them, you automatically affirm, "I have this thing."

Sewing, Needlework, and Fabric Crafts

Fabric crafts such as sewing, crochet, knitting, embroidery, beading, rug hooking, macrame, and others can be adapted to magical purposes. These crafts can be used to make practical items like clothing, accessories, quilts, or banners. Natural, as opposed to synthetic, materials and fibers respond best to magical uses. Projects of this nature are especially appropriate for magic used to attract love, a cozy home life, security, and happiness.

Fabric crafts can be more limited in their range of designs and depictions than many other art forms. However, stitchery, knotting, hooking, and other motions involve conscious actions that can be used to imprint the Unconscious with magical suggestions. With each stitch or other motion you make, you can also impress psychic energy into the project and direct it toward a magical objective. The repetitious and rhythmic nature of crafts such as spinning, weaving, and crocheting can put you into a semi-hypnotic state, which is also conducive to imprinting the Unconscious.

Many of the designs and patterns used in quilting, applique, and embroidery make use of geometric shapes and other symbols that call upon archetypal powers, and can be used to depict qualities and things you want to bring into your life. For example, the popular sunburst designs evoke the radiant solar qualities of richness, expansiveness, and creativity. Many of these symbols are ancient. (Refer to Appendix III for basic symbolic meanings of some of these popular geometric designs.)

If you would like to learn more about the magical connotations of various crafts including spinning, embroidery, quilting, and many others, Paula Campanelli provides a rich trove of information in her book, *Wheel of the Year.*[3]

Jewelry Making

When you experiment with making jewelry, you have an opportunity to work with many colorful and wonderful natural materials. The creating and wearing of beautiful things for personal adornment taps into the same inner reserves of power and mystery that fascinated our paleolithic ancestors. In using your imagination to craft personal decorations, you can bring inner drama into a tangible form, even if only in something small and fragile. The use of jewelry is one of the most popular ways in which mystically attuned people like to make magical statements.

As you might expect, jewelry, jewels, and jewelry making are steeped in magical lore. If you get into working with jewelry in any degree, you'll soon find yourself picking up a lot of this lore, and using it to inspire your own designs.

Jewelry has long been among the proprietary objects of the Love Goddess, who has been known as Venus, Aphrodite, Freya, Erzulie, Oshun, Bast, Astarte, and by many other names. Thus, the making and use of jewelry invokes Her presence. I've found that there's no way around it, at least in my own experience. When I work with things of beauty, especially jewels and related items, She makes herself known, even if there was no magical or sensual intent. It follows that this would be a good magical activity for people who want to bring love and romance into their lives.

Charms are one of the best known uses of jewelry in magic. Since charms are essentially symbols, you can refer to Appendix III to learn more about the magical meanings of some of the symbols that are commonly used as charms.

It's interesting to note that beaded necklaces are often represented on the ancient, primitive figurines and carvings known as "Eye Goddesses," which are found from Asia to Northern Europe. Though roughly sculptured and not well detailed, they generally have three common characteristics: eyes, breasts, and a necklace of beads. Joan Mowat Erikson, an expert on bead lore, has a theory about this, saying:

> If primitive and infantile experience can be related to one another—and much speaks for this assumption—then this ancient deity may be described as the infant's-eye view mother goddess, for her attributes are those within the infant's cognitive universe.[4]

She feels that the beads are part of this image because there's something in the brightness and roundness of beads that reminds the primitive mind of eyes. Mowat also suggests that mothers have used their beads to stimulate and comfort their babes when their own eyes are temporarily diverted. This is supported by the fact that "eye beads" are widespread as magical amulets and talismans. There is also the art of "fascination," which refers to different magical techniques generally involving the use of bright shiny jewelry objects coupled with well planned physical maneuvers to attract the opposite sex and bring them under your influence. In all of these things, we see a connection between the realm of the erotic and some ingrained, primitive human responses.

There's a lot more to be said about the use of jewelry in magic, but that would digress too far from the subject of this book. One more point I would like to make is that the motions that go into jewelry making, beading in particular, are therapeutic, combining relaxing rhythmic actions with stimulating ideas and objects. This is an excellent therapy to indulge in when you're either too wired or too worried.

Miscellaneous Arts and Crafts

If you've read about all the above art and craft options, it should now be apparent that the same principles apply to any other crafts you may want to engage in, such as woodcarving, metalworking, nature crafts, basket weaving, stained glass, and all others. Basically, you can turn crafts into magical spells by using both actual and symbolic designs and images as affirmations of what you want to bring into your life, and by combining actions and motions with focused psychic energy.

Endnotes

1. Campbell, Joseph. *The Flight of the Wild Gander.* Washington, D.C.: Gateway, 1951.

2. Wolfe, Amber. *In the Shadow of the Shaman.* St. Paul: LLewellyn, 1989.

3. Campanelli, Pauline. *Wheel of the Year, Living the Magical Life.* St. Paul: LLewellyn, 1989.

4. Erikson, Joan Mowat. *The Universal Bead.* New York: Norton, 1969.

Chapter 11

Magical Playthings

Even though most of you readers are probably adults, or at least young adults, you may very well have kept some of your childhood toys around. Perhaps they are collectors' items, or maybe they just have decorative or sentimental value. Indeed, a lot of people continue to collect various types of toys because they appeal for a number of personal reasons. Even for adults, having things to toy around with relieves stress and also provides that type of "stew-around" play that activates the right brain's creativity. Play and playthings are also used in many forms of therapy. Since toys are important to play, they certainly have a part in playful magic.

Handling, playing, and working with toys involves the active use of imagination, and encourages us to be silly and to try new modes of acting. Also, when you make or construct the toys yourself, you give your hands something to do that's relaxing and satisfying. As a hobby, toy collecting is a way to indulge your

curiosity, and is especially helpful to persons who have lost interest in their daily routine or line of work.

When you make the toys you collect or play with, you consciously or unconsciously make an affirmation that you are the shaper of your own reality. Toy making or assembling involves the same magical principles discussed in Chapter 10, which looked at arts and handcrafts. Doing things with your hands and body activates more areas of your brain and has the spiritual effect of engaging more aspects of your being. With certain types of miniatures, such as doll houses, model railroads, and other types of dioramas, you are especially making the statement, "I have the power to create my own world." The arranging and moving around of all of the little pieces makes a statement that you are in control of your world, that you can act on your surroundings. You construct an idealized microcosm where elements are integrated into a harmonious whole, suggesting that all is well, all is balanced and in control in the macrocosm of your world and your life.

Making, acquiring, assembling, displaying, and just enjoying certain toys can be rich in magical symbolism which affirms the things you would like to have in your life, whether they stand for simple material things or abstract concepts. You can acquire a toy or buy something for your doll house or model railroad that is a miniature of or akin to something that you want. You thereby affirm, "I have this thing." There can be additional symbolism bound up in the actual structure and appearance of the playthings, so they can also act as lucky charms. (Refer to Appendix III.)

On a deeper level, toys could certainly be used as tools for personal transformation and self-fulfillment, based on the old magical belief that to make or acquire the symbol of a thing is to have that thing or its quality. Certainly, the reason some adults are deeply attracted to particular dolls or other toys is because they hold some deeper personal meanings for those individuals. If you happen to be walking past the toy store and see something in the window that you "just gotta have," you might reach inside of yourself or consult various studies on symbolism to explore the reason. What does it tell you about yourself? I think these things have particular meaning to the Deep Self and its desire for actualization. For this reason, it has become common for therapists to urge their patients to keep dolls, teddy bears, and the like, as a means of helping them focus on certain needs; for example, the need to love and nourish that inner child.

The types of toys you're attracted to can be a key to your personal purpose and inner vitality. Ask yourself what sort of play occupied most of your childhood hours. Picture yourself as the child you once were, and then look down at your hands. What would you be holding in your hands? What would you be doing with your hands and body? What type of area or setting would you most likely be playing in? Just as the growth of a crystal follows a seemingly invisible template and an acorn knows it has to be an oak, a child instinctively knows what its True Self is meant to be. The pressures from our families and society are like the forces that distort the crystal or smother the seedling. Recalling the child you were is one way to rediscover who you were meant to be, and looking at your hands is another.

The thing that most naturally finds its way into your hands is the staff of your power. The thing that a child takes into his or her hands gives a clue to his or her destiny. This also carries a warning. There is a scene in the movie, *Witness,* where an Amish

grandfather warns a little boy to stay away from guns, saying, "What you take into your hands, you also take into your heart." Abraham Lincoln realized this. As a young man, he was confused and depressed about which direction to take in his life. He remembered the biblical instance when God prompted Moses to strike water with his staff by asking him, "What is that in thine hand?" In Lincoln's case, it was the pen he was holding in his hand which transfixed him with the realization that his was the power to change the world with words. On a similar principle, when Carl Jung went through a depression, he remembered that, as a child, he had loved to build little castles of sand, mud, and stones. He discovered he was able to reconnect with the source of his joy and vitality by working on his own house with his own hands.

Jean Jacques Rousseau wrote that young people should be given things to do with their hands, delaying the more abstract forms of education until later. He felt this would be calming and centering, enabling them to better deal with all of the conflicts that come up in adolescence.

However, parents and educators haven't always been too interested in what Rousseau had to say. My dad recalls that when he was a young man, in the late forties and through the fifties, there was a movement afoot to dissuade young people from going into the trades and to direct them toward office careers. The philosophy was that if you see a kid pick up a tool, slap his hand with a ruler and replace the tool with a pencil, so he'll become an accountant. Dad feels that this movement contributed to America's loss of industrial and manufacturing preeminence. Around the same time this was happening, Americans stopped making their own toys. They gave this job away to others. Perhaps by taking back our toys, we can take back our power, collectively and individually.

So much for the social lecture. To return to the subject of recalling your childhood playthings—it's not just the nature of the toy that tells you something, but the way you played with it. Give the same doll to ten different children, and they'll play with it ten different ways. One will interact with it in a nurturing manner; one will picture it as an adventurer in exotic lands; one will build little rooms, houses and other structures for it; and so on. So when you think about the way you played as a child, think about the mode of play and the energies you expressed.

The other magical principle that's tied in with the use of toys is animism. With frequent use, toys do seem to take on a life of their own, to become artificial elementals, so to speak. Psychic, as well as psychological, factors result in the transference of Life Force. Because they are so imbued with life, the presence of toys confers liveliness.

For this reason, I feel that both adults and children should limit themselves to relatively few toys, and those should be carefully selected and of good quality. This is not because there is any danger in animating toys, but rather because it's so sad to see them abandoned and left to go dormant after their owners have lost interest in them. (Children don't need a lot of store-bought toys anyway—you'll find that they can engage in creative play with such things as plastic kitchen implements, wood and fabric scraps, common household objects, and natural objects like shells and pine cones.) Along with this, there is an ethical and ecological principle inherent in making toys out of recycled and scrap materials, as well as trying to repair toys instead of junking them and buying new ones.

Some magicians consciously create their own artificial elementals (i.e. familiars), by imbuing toys with psychic power. Usually this is done with some end in mind, charging the spirit of that toy with a particular task. Of course, you don't have to feel that your animate toys need to be "put to work" for anything. You can just show your appreciation for their companionship by getting them out once in a while. Try throwing a tea party for your dolls and stuffed animals, or clean and polish those little cars and trucks and set them out on display.

Playthings for Pragmatically Magical Purposes

With the above principles in mind, we can turn our use and enjoyment of toy objects into positive affirmations or magical spells by adding a magical intent, along with appropriate visualizations and affirmations. All of these physical and mental activities send more power to your magical goals. When you start to gather your toys together and work on them or play with them, the amount of ceremony you put into it is up to you—although, as I've said, just handling them is, in and of itself, a magical act. If you wish to add some ritual to toy making or arranging, look at the rite for starting and finishing art and handicrafts projects in Chapter 10; you can modify the words and visualizations to fit whatever type of toys you are working with and to suit whatever purpose you have in mind. Following are some common toys that you can imbue with magical meaning.

Doll Houses

A doll house can be used as a magical affirmation for many good things: security, prosperity, and a happy home life. Doll houses can also be used toward some pragmatic magical ends: attracting your dream house into your life, getting a good deal on a house, or helping sell the house you have.

If you make a doll house with the magical intent to manifest a dream house, remember, in putting together the doll house, you're not necessarily stipulating that the dream house will look or be laid out exactly like that, but rather, your creation represents a place that will meet your needs and give you the quality of life you want. You can incorporate the physical features you're looking for into the doll house. A dream house incorporates ideals, such as security and domestic happiness, and personal physical requirements, such as a pantry or fireplace. With the creation of a doll house, there's the affirmation that you have your ideal home. It's right; it's meant to be—so it's more likely to bring in the synchronicities that will lead you to the right place and help you get a good deal on it.

When the magical goal is to help you sell a house, the actual contents of the doll house need be less personally significant than when you're doing this to find your dream house or satisfy personal needs. You do want doll furnishings that suggest comfort and tradition, like detailed miniature baked goods, pets, etc. For this purpose, anoint the doll house miniatures with essential oils such as vanilla, which is said to attract domestic love and happiness, and will create those associations in the mind of the potential buyer. (Do small patch tests first, in case any of the miniatures might be made of materials that could get sticky or stained by certain oils.) Have the doll house well displayed so potential buyers will notice it when they enter your house. This will have both a magical and psychological effect on them.

I enjoy working on doll houses myself. It's something I do just for fun, magic isn't my intent. I am aware of the magic inherent in it and haven't bothered to use any ritual actions. Nevertheless, my hobby may have served the purpose of a spell and gotten good results—helping me in the buying and selling of a home. I found a dream house (or what was a dream house for me at that time), even though I wasn't out looking for one. The acquisition of the house was facilitated by the fact that it was in the same price range as my prior home, which we sold on its first day on the market.

Dolls

Because dolls are actually miniature representations of humans, their symbolic attraction can be quite strong. It's no wonder many adults are devoted doll collectors. And there's such a wide range of doll types available these days! You can find stuffed animals, puppets, and paper dolls, exquisitely dressed in imaginative costumes.

For psychological purposes, dolls provide a certain type of wish fulfillment. Some doll symbolism is pretty obvious: a wish to have and to nurture children, and also to express one's femininity. That's why the majority of doll collectors are childless women, or women who have only male children and have thus gotten out of touch with a lot of the little things that are seen as traditional feminine values and interests.

Some feminists have run this gamut of rejecting the so-called traditional feminine characteristics due to societal associations with weakness and incompetence. These women are now reclaiming these "soft" qualities as a way of finding pleasure in their own bodies and persons, and are taking an interest in doll collecting or are bringing out the dolls of their childhood as a way of regaining contact with this fragment of the Self. In the women's spirituality movement, there are rituals where women make dolls or bring their favorite dolls to group sessions. They talk about them, play with them, and let them interact with each other in imaginative ways.[1]

Some collectors may be attracted to dolls that resemble themselves as children, either in looks or expression, or that convey some valued or wistful quality. In so doing, one can relate to the inner child of the past, or to the child archetype, which is transpersonal. There have been some jokes about New Agers and "self-love" dolls, but caring for a doll is a valid therapeutic technique for bringing out self-nurturing qualities.

For practical magical purposes, dolls can be used in imitative magic. Getting a doll that looks like you and making clothes, jewelry, or furnishings for it symbolizes that good things will be attracted to you. (This is a positive use of the old-fashioned voodoo doll.) So, if you still have your childhood dolls, get out your old collection and make or buy them some new accessories. This is a statement to affirm good new things coming into your own life.

Making and dressing dolls can also help you sort out personal issues, because, as you put the dolls together and decide what you want them to look like and how you want to dress them, you're consciously and unconsciously sorting out priorities and making decisions. There's going to be a tendency to endow those dolls with characteristics and qualities you value—ones that you have, or ones your deeper consciousness recognizes a need to develop.

Elemental Toys

In Chapter 4, the discussion of playful personalities looked at elemental characteristics. You can use play as a way of experiencing the energies of and identifying with the elements of Earth, Air, Fire, and Water. As you may expect, the individual elements have affinities with certain types of toys. Electric trains, cars, and, in fact, all electronic toys, have the active qualities of the Fire element. Elemental Air is represented in balloons, balls, whistles, darts and other target items, and toy airplanes, as well as all games and toys that call on mental qualities. Earth toys are marbles and jacks; doll houses, model train settings, and other dioramas; dolls, teddy bears, and other stuffed animals; building blocks and construction sets; and clay and other materials used to give substance to playthings. Elemental Water is invoked with the use of toy boats and items for pouring such as cups and pitchers, and it also covers the use of paints and fluid materials. Because of its emotional qualities, elemental Water is also associated with dolls and stuffed animals, as there is a tendency to project a lot of emotion into them. Following, is a simplified chart to give you an overview of the magical potential of toys, as related to the four elements.

ELEMENT	TYPES OF TOYS	ASSOCIATIONS AND SHAMANIC TOTEMS
FIRE	*battery powered and electric toys* *trains, cars, trucks* *toy soldiers, action figures* *play kitchens and their accessories* *cap guns* *some video games* *sports accessories*	*Aries, Leo, Sagittarius* *the Southern quarter* *times: noon and summer* *colors: red and orange* *elementals: salamanders* *magical tools: candles and wands* *magical intent: energizing*
EARTH	*craft kits, tools* *wood, paper, clay* *marbles, jacks, and tiddlywinks* *doll houses, dioramas, and miniatures* *model train layouts* *building blocks* *construction sets* *natural science kits* *garden toys and farm sets* *sand boxes*	*Taurus, Virgo, Capricorn* *the Northern quarter* *times: midnight and winter* *colors: brown, green, black* *elementals: gnomes* *magical tools: stones, bones crystals, fossils, pentacles* *magical intent: security and grounding*

ELEMENT	TYPES OF TOYS	ASSOCIATIONS AND SHAMANIC TOTEMS
AIR	balloons, balls, kites whistles and musical toys darts and target toys airplanes board games role playing games some video games cards and dice puppets costumes and accessories for pretending party favors playground sets: swings and slides kaleidoscopes	Gemini, Libra, Aquarius the Eastern quarter times: dawn and spring colors: yellow, white, and light blue elementals: sylphs magical tools: feathers, mirrors, masks, bells, blades, and incense magical intent: creativity and mental stimulation
WATER	boats beach and tub toys miniature cups, pitchers, tea sets paints dolls and stuffed animals doll accessories soap bubble makers	Cancer, Scorpio, Pisces the Western quarter times: sunset and fall colors: blue and green elementals: undines magical tools: shells and goblets magical intent: emotional enrichment

The elemental associations can be helpful in finding ways to invite the development of new facets of your Self, and they're something to bear in mind when choosing toys for children. (Refer to Chapter 4 for more information on recognizing, augmenting, and balancing the elemental personality types.[2]) The magical intent is also an important consideration in selecting toys.

How you arrange or display your toys can also have meaning. The usual method is to group them according to physical type, but using the elemental associations suggests additional ways to classify them. You could put toys relating to the Earth element in a grouping with other Earth symbols. You can also make groupings based on elemental color associations, as well as other magical color associations (Refer to Appendix I for more information on the symbolism of color.), using monochrome schemes or mixtures of colors to get the desired effects. Lighting is also important. It can be used to enhance color, and the reflection of light has magical and psychological effects. Toys can also be arranged in geometric patterns or by the geometric forms they take. (Refer to Appendix III for more information on geometrical symbolism.) And, of course, when you do things with magical intent, the posing and juxtaposition of such items as dolls, stuffed animals, and action figures can be significant.

Playtime

Beyond the types of play suggested by toys' conventional uses, plus the acquisition and various uses of toys with magical intent as mentioned throughout this chapter, there are possibilities for new types of creative and magical play.

An example of such an innovative pastime is Elven Chess as developed and described by Diane Darling and Eldri Littlewolf.[3] For this game, participants bring or gather their interesting and wonderful little objects, spread them on the designated "board," which can be a rug, cloth, or table top, then sit in a circle while they take turns laying them out in whatever patterns they feel moved to make. Moves progress clockwise, and a turn consists of up to three moves, which may be of "addition, subtraction, or relocation, in any dimensional plane." The authors say, "There are no accidents in Elven Chess. The cat, a caterpillar crossing the board, a ferret stealing the rubber cockroach, all count as moves. Especially beautiful moves are applauded and praised softly." It's OK for players to move each others' objects, though they should wait one turn before changing someone else's move. There are few rules, the game ends when everyone is finished, and everybody wins.

Toys themselves can suggest magical interactions. A lot of totem relationships, as described by Amber Wolfe in *In the Shadow of the Shaman,* are very playful in nature, which suggests toys as totems, and totems as toys.[4]

I hope this chapter will inspire you to develop some new forms of play and uses for playthings. Here are just a few possibilities:

- drama and pretend

- enlivening the work place

- unconventional toys and creative play

- using natural materials in playthings and play

- scrap and recycled materials turned into playthings

- playful interactions with friends and lovers

- play that energizes different chakras

- exchange of playful energy with the Faery Realm

- play that opens a connection with ancestor spirits

- play to explore Earth mysteries

- using toys in seasonal celebrations

- experiencing children's energies by participation in their games

- encouraging children to create new forms of play

In concluding this chapter, it's interesting to note that a number of traditional games and playthings have quasi-magical origins. The history of playthings and pastimes is one of the most fascinating branches of folklore and folk life, and worth looking into more deeply.[5]

Endnotes

1. For an example of how dolls may be used in women's spirituality, refer to *Women's Rituals* by Barbara Walker (San Francisco: Harper and Row, 1990).

2. As an engaging gift for a child, I suggest getting a cigar box or some other interesting box and filling it with small but colorful and interesting toy objects, natural objects such as shells and crystals, and other curious things, seeing that all the elements are represented. It's also an interesting sort of a thing to have on hand to amuse children who come to visit you. I had an aunt who had a box like that, and I was always fascinated by its contents, which included a geode.

3. Darling, Diane, and Littlewolf, Eldri. *"Elven Chess: A Game for All Seasons," The Green Egg, v.XXII*, No. 87, Samhain, 1989. Ukiah: POB 1542.

4. Wolfe, Amber. *In the Shadow of the Shaman.* St. Paul: Llewellyn, 1988.

5. For more information on the role of games in magic (including the Earth mysteries), read *Games of the Gods* by Nigel Pennick (York Beach: Weiser, 1989).

Chapter 12

Playing Under the Moon Signs

A special quality of magic comes into our lives when we are willing to do things spontaneously, break routine, make time for play, and try new things. Those of us who have a tendency to get too deeply rooted in routine may initially have to make a conscious effort and "plan" to be spontaneous!

Intuition should be our number one guide in coming up with things to do. If an idea pops into your head or you feel there's something special you'd like to do, go for it, and don't procrastinate. It's also important to allow yourself to be open to suggestion, for there are many potential channels of guidance: family, friends, the media, trends, unfolding events, and so on. In addition, astrology teaches us that certain activities can be especially rewarding when the Moon is transiting through certain signs of the zodiac. She enters a new sign every 2 to 2 ½ days, and with each successive transit, new and different moods, influences, and opportunities make themselves felt. Engaging in activities which are favored

by the transit can mean you're more likely to be doing things or being in places where the tides of power can carry you along, or put you in sync with the cosmic energies and enable you to be in the right time and the right place for magical and serendipitous things to happen.

Most almanacs will tell you which sign the Moon is in for any given day, and a number of calendars now include that information. Llewellyn Publications publishes annual guides including the *Sun Sign Book, Moon Sign Book, Daily Planetary Guide, Astrological Calendar,* and *Magical Almanac,* all of which feature Moon sign information.[1]

Here are suggestions for fun activities that bring out the qualities of spontaneity, curiosity, and fantasy, and can be especially meaningful when the Moon is in the following signs of the Zodiac.

Moon in Aries

The Moon's transit through Aries is auspicious for bold, decisive action, and impulsive, spontaneous activities. Therefore, you can feel more empowered to undertake any activity which calls for you to make a major break with your routine and your normal way of doing things. You might find inspiration in the words of Goethe, who said, "Whatever you believe you can do or dream you can, begin it. Boldness has genius, power, and magic."

Energies run high when the Moon is in Aries, so take advantage and join in sports and other physically intense pursuits. Go dancing. Aries is ruled by Mars, and dancing is actually a traditional expression, as well as psychological outlet, of Mars energy. Or, explore the martial arts or other sports or art forms that celebrate action, movement, and bodily grace and agility.

Become more aware of scientific and metaphysical theories about energy, then see if you can detect patterns of energy in the things going on in the physical world around you.

Aries is also concerned with glorification of the self and the needs of the ego. Try repeating affirmations that give your ego a massive boost. (See Appendix IV on affirmations.) Don't worry about sounding conceited, it's good for your mental health.

Moon in Taurus

Transiting through Taurus, the Moon is said to be exalted, for she is very much in harmony with Venus, Taurus' ruler. This stirs feelings of love and longing. It is an especially appropriate time to be with a lover. You might invite your lover to join in some of the suggestions for celebrating the five senses mentioned below.

This transit heightens our appreciation for physical comfort, so devote time to luxuries that pamper the body and please the senses. Take a long, relaxing bath using fragrant, quality bath oils. For atmosphere, burn incense, bathe by candlelight, and have classical or New Age music playing. Treat yourself to a massage, a beauty treatment, or some other pleasurable form of therapy. Revel in the healing and nurturing power of touch.

In keeping with Taurus' appreciation of the senses, study aromas. Learn about aromatherapy and explore the magical uses of incenses, oils, perfumes, herbs, flowers, and powders which involve a variety of fragrances.[2] You may find that working with ingredients such as herbs, flowers, oils, and other natural materials is energizing because they're so concentrated with Life Force. Visit the perfume counter at your local department store and try out some of the different fragrances. Fill your home with scent by burning incense and making your own pomanders, potpourris, and sachets.

Indulge the Love Goddess' pleasure in cosmetic beauty products, personal ornamentation, or grooming products. You can avoid the impulse to spend too much on these little luxuries—which is also a tendency of this transit—by consulting herbals and other how-to books that provide recipes for making your own.

Taurus is considered the most food loving of signs, so if you don't need to watch your weight, treat yourself to a lavish and exotic dessert. Get some friends together, go trooping through a variety of restaurants, ethnic delicatessens, and specialty food stores. Sample or acquire something from each place. If you need to count calories, stick with stimulating the senses of touch, smell, hearing, and sight, as mentioned. (You can indulge in some of the more interesting diet and health foods available. In the past, luxury food meant sweet and fatty, today it means quality or gourmet.)

Taurus is at home in the countryside, so this is a great time to go for a long drive down some back country roads. Take leisurely walks through fields and woodlots. Visit cider mills or orchards where you can pick your own fruit. A tour of wine cellars would be appropriate. Attend a country fair or craft show. Gratify Taurus' love of beautiful objects by stopping in rural antique shops. Have dinner in a quaint country inn with folk or traditional music, or cap the evening with country music and entertainment.

Moon in Gemini

As the sign that favors communication, travel, and mental games, the Moon's transit through Gemini is just full of opportunities for playful people.

One of Mercury's best qualities is getting around, so go take a ride. Use a form of transportation you've never tried or you seldom use, such as a train, ferry, steamboat, or even a hot air balloon.

This is a time for getting in touch and staying in touch. Go to a large card shop and pick out humorous or meaningful greeting cards to send to your friends and relatives, or design your own greetings. You don't need a special occasion to say Hi. Call a friend—particularly one you've been out of touch with—and propose to go on some adventurous outing.

Gemini's ruler, Mercury, is the patron of gamesters and tricksters. Play practical jokes. But make sure they are pranks your friends will find amusing and humorous; don't do anything mean-spirited. Have an impromptu gathering of friends for an evening of board games, especially ones that challenge the mind or stimulate the wit. If you have an addiction for video and computer games, you can justify it at this time. Mercury encourages games which emphasize speedy reflexes and hand-eye coordination.

This is the ideal time for free expression, so try your hand at creative writing. Try composing songs and poems, designing a children's book, or starting a journal. Learn to appreciate verbal techniques by listening to a professional storyteller, or have a storytelling session with your friends or family.

As part of his communicative function, Mercury (Hermes to the Greeks) was associated with oracles. The Greeks believed that Hermes could make the future and other matters known through randomly spoken words that, when overheard, could have significant personal meanings. Therefore, when the Moon is transiting through this sign, you might try making a game of listening to the cross-talk around you, seeing what words seem to jump out at you, and examining them to see if there's a meaningful pattern.

Mercury is associated with spontaneity and serendipitous occurrences. Without any planning or forethought, take a walk or drive to some unfamiliar place without thinking about what you're going to do or having any expectations of what you're going to see when you get there. Be open, observant, take time to chat with any strangers you meet, and detach yourself from time pressures or the idea that everything has to have a purpose.

Moon in Cancer

The Moon is in close affinity with the world of Nature and her primal energies. Since the Moon is at home in Cancer, in her own element, this is an ideal time to attune oneself with the rhythms of Nature. Break from your routine to connect with Nature by going barefoot, hugging trees, walking in summer rain, etc. For extra zest, go to some especially dramatic and magical natural spot, such as a waterfall, mountainside, seashore, or ancient grove.

Family feelings run strong when the Moon is in Cancer, so include your loved ones in any special activities you pursue. Choose "heart activities"—things you do together that synchronize your thoughts and actions. These will put you in emotional attunement. Along with this comes an awareness of the importance of nurturing and caring for loved ones. You can take special pleasure in doing things to serve your family, such as preparing wholesome and comforting meals, giving backrubs, and so on. Remember, you need to be nurtured too, so ask for help when you need it. If you have kids, instruct them in doing small things to help prepare and serve a meal, or some other household task. When everybody contributes something, a type of "synergy" takes place—each person gets more energy out of it than he or she put into it.

Since this strong Moon position heightens sentiment, spend time reading and writing poetry and focusing on other things that honor the finer emotions. Be generous with sincere compliments and tell your loved ones how you feel about them. Don't be afraid to speak from the heart. Sometimes we think this unnecessary because we assume that our loved ones should already know how we feel. In actuality, these things can never be said often enough.

Cancer bestows a great love of home, so try your hand at redecorating. Have fun and be whimsical. Decorating for upcoming holidays is something you can throw yourself into.

This is a highly fertile period, so try your hand at gardening. Many people find that working with plants and the Earth gives them a sense of deep contentment and renewal.

Moon in Leo

The Moon in Leo creates a love of entertaining and of being entertained, of drama and being dramatic, so there are a lot of ways to use these impulses creatively.

Call your friends together for an impromptu party, or go somewhere where people get together to party. Let your desire to keep things lively overcome your inhibitions. The Moon in Leo prompts us to show off our talents, so go to a night club that has an amateur night where you can sing, act, or tell jokes. Or organize a talent show for your friends.

Express yourself artistically and at the same time explore the drama of your multiple inner selves by making masks. Some craft stores sell mask making kits, or you can devise simple ones of your own from scrap materials. Incorporate sequins, glitter, feathers, beads, or whatever you desire. As an alternative to mask making, experiment with face painting. Mask making and face painting sessions are something to turn into a party. Drag out any costume pieces you have or likely materials for make-shift costumes, then have an impromptu masquerade.

Try out new personas in public or among friends. If you happen to be going out somewhere, how about putting on a bit? See if you can pretend to be someone you're not—perhaps a bolder person, a younger or older person, a foreigner, etc.

Honor Leo's ruler, the Sun, by getting up earlier than usual. Watch the diffuse sunlight painting the dawning sky with color. Those who study Prana (the Life Force) say that it is especially

strong in the morning. You can literally drink it in by stepping out-side to breathe the vital morning air and experience the energies of the rising Sun and awakening Earth. Take an early morning walk and enjoy the sight of the gradual stirring of both the human and animal inhabitants of your world.

Moon in Virgo

When the Moon is in Virgo, we tend to be conscious of bodily health and dietary concerns. You can take advantage of this in a fun way by trying your hand at some creative, healthful cooking. Try specialty recipes or ethnic cuisine. Put an emphasis on fresh-ness, wholesomeness, and purity of ingredients. Make a trip to a health food store and try something that's new or exotic. Or go out to eat at a quality ethnic or health food restaurant where you can take in nutrition while enjoying ambience.

The Moon's transit through Virgo harmonizes with the Earth Powers. Experiment with "green magic", including the lore of herbs, homeopathy, and the healing powers of nature. Spend time doing some gardening, and familiarize yourself with different types of plants. Discover how you can interact with the Life Force by working with greenery and living things: try making floral arrange-ments, wreaths, etc. Practice identifying the flora in your area, and learn how they are used in nutrition, healing, folklore and magic.

Make the most of Virgo's nurturing qualities by bringing some cheer to sick friends or shut-in neighbors. Take them chicken soup or flowers, or have some jokes or gossip to tell. This is also a good time to pay attention to your own health. Try to "get in touch" with your body, which too many of us take for granted. Experi-ment with the healing or healthful arts and therapies such as crys-tal power, applied kinesiology, tai chi, reiki, Feldenkrais, etc.[3]

Virgo is the sign most concerned with work, so to be in keeping with playful magic, use your imagination to devise ways to turn chores and rote work into games that boost your efficiency. The

Moon's transit through Virgo bestows a greater ability to focus on detail work, so this would be a good time to become absorbed in any intricate handicrafts. Check to see if your local recreation department or community college is offering any workshops that will enable you to learn a new form of handicraft. Crafts, especially those of a rhythmic nature such as knitting and crochet, can center you as well as give you a sense of inner satisfaction.

Moon in Libra

When the Moon is in Libra, the sign that likes to bring people together, focus on romance, partnerships, and friendships. Include a friend or lover in any interesting projects or playful activities you become involved in at this time.

Light-hearted flirting is very much encouraged when the Moon is in Libra. This will give you a chance to practice projecting personal charm, wit, graciousness, and style.

Entertain an intimate gathering of your closest friends. Allowing your ingenuity to be stimulated by the energies of this transit, create an atmosphere of elegance and beauty. Have soft lighting and play beautiful music. You could have an impromptu, but graceful, tea party with your best china and some very delicate cakes or cookies from the bakery. This is an opportunity to create timeless moments that will leave lasting memories.

The Moon in Libra stirs a desire to surround oneself with art and beauty, so this is an excellent time to engage in any kind of creative pursuits. Visit an art show or gallery. Consider starting one of the magical art projects suggested in Chapter 10. You will be able to draw deeply on your inner inspiration, bringing your own ideal of beauty to your artistic efforts.

Because aesthetic awareness is heightened, this is also a good time to explore and refine your senses. One thing you might consider is experimenting with the uses of essential oils—for massage, beauty, aromatherapy, potpourri, and magic.

Moon in Scorpio

The Moon's transit through Scorpio intensifies all experiences. This is sometimes considered negative, but you can turn it positive by planning experiences that are upbeat and creative.

Scorpio loves high drama and emotional extravagance, so this is an ideal time to take in live drama—attend an opera, musical, or play. When you're alone or in the company of supportive friends, make up dances to express your emotions, symbolize your desires, or reenact a dream or special experience. Go all out putting together costumes and accessories for your dances, such as veils, masks, swords, fans, etc. Make music to accompany your dance; try finger cymbals, rattles, bells, etc. Consider buying or making a new piece of jewelry or clothing that enables you to be in touch with your dramatic, darkly mysterious, or wildly romantic side.

The intensity of physical and emotional experience heightens sexual desire, so this is the time to plan to be alone with a lover.

Scorpio has an affinity with the night side of nature, so make friends with the night. Venture out for moonlit drives or walks. (Evening strolls are one of the many reasons for appreciating warm summer nights.) Watch the world and its inhabitants as they retire to rest. Observe the creatures that emerge at night. Study the different tones and textures of darkness. Listen to nocturnal sounds. Taste and sniff the air. Pay attention to the night sky. What phase of the Moon is it? Which stars and constellations are prominent? Stop by all-night restaurants or stores and observe your fellow humans who are up and around at that time too. One word of warning: this transit can heighten attraction to danger, so make sure any nighttime roving is done in fairly safe areas.

Scorpio is also concerned with generation, so this can be a good time look for fun ways to explore your own roots by going through family photographs and documents, retelling your family's stories, and visiting past family sites or going to culture centers, restaurants, and festivals that celebrate your own ethnic heritage. If you have deeper metaphysical training, this can be an opportunity to align yourself with ancestral energies and access the dreaming time of your family and race.

Moon in Sagittarius

The Moon's transit through Sagittarius stirs a restlessness that is best satisfied by outdoor activities and adventures, including sports and travel. Because this transit makes for expansive and socially outgoing tendencies coupled with a desire for action, organize your friends for a game of softball or croquet, or other outdoor activities.

Sagittarius gives an affinity for animals, wildlife, and natural settings, so this is an appropriate time to visit a wildlife refuge, nature park, or zoo. Look for opportunities to interact with animals. The horse, of course, is Sagittarius' favorite animal, so plan a trip to a riding stable or dude ranch where you can interact with your equine friends.

Sagittarius takes a philosophical interest in other people. Go to the mall to do some people watching. When you meet friends or strangers, observe and listen to what they have to say about themselves. Participate in volunteer activities that enable you to work with a wide spectrum of people.

When the Moon is in Sagittarius, you can become concerned with deep philosophical and religious matters, including the forms and trappings of organized religion. Do things to strengthen your own religious interests and spirituality. If you are not a member of a traditional or organized religion, you may want to view or participate in some of the pageantry or ceremony of a local church or temple. This is also a good time to learn more about alternative religions.

Moon in Capricorn

Capricorn is the most solemn and serious sign of the zodiac. The Moon is at her detriment when she makes this transit, so do anything you can to infuse such a day with laughter and lightheartedness. Try any of the suggestions given for any of the other signs here, just to offset the tendency toward depression and moodiness. Surround yourself with humor. Read comic books and trade jokes. Watch children's cartoons. Go to a comedy movie or rent one.

Capricorn's influence can make us focus too much on the cares and responsibilities of age. When the Moon is in this sign, take your children (if you have them), or else some younger relatives or neighbors to the park or on some enjoyable outing so you can catch their enthusiasm and experience their pleasure vicariously.

Today there is a lot of discussion and literature available on bringing out the inner child, so look into this subject. Get out your old childhood photos, and see how visibly you used to express exuberant energy, lightheartedness, and trust. Doesn't just looking at those photos impress you with how much that beautiful little child deserves all the best things life has to give? You can also connect with your inner child of the past by going through your old toys, if you still have them. In keeping with the animistic view-point which states that things have personalities, or at least can acquire some with prolonged use, honor the toys of your childhood by playing with them again or by cleaning and displaying them. Just for the heck of it, decorate your main room or private quarters with balloons, streamers, and paper garlands, as if you were planning a children's party.

At the same time, the Saturnine influence can also help you value the wisdom of age, as well as feel more empathy for the elderly. This is an excellent time to visit elderly friends or relatives. If they feel like talking about the Great Depression or how tough they had it when they were young, ask them what they did for entertainment. What kind of innovative toys or play did they invent in order to have a good time in the middle of hard times?

This is a sign which preaches hard work and endurance, so go do some people watching where workers carry out their duties in interesting environments, such as ports of call or construction sites.

Capricorn's connection with the structure of the Earth makes this a good time to appreciate the beauty and explore the powers of the Mineral World and Earth Element. Visit mines, caves, mountains, and places where the presence of the Earth Powers is heavy, or visit rock shows, crystal shops, and natural history museums to learn more about gemstones and geological phenomena.

Moon in Aquarius

When the Moon enters Aquarius, it stirs a genuine interest in the ways and ideas of other people, and it places a high value on social interactions. Find any excuse for a gathering and invite your friends over, or go to the places where your kind of people hang out. People watching also satisfies some of the curiosity aroused by this transit. Go to a busy public place to observe the smorgasbord of people and their activities, or take in some performance art or live music.

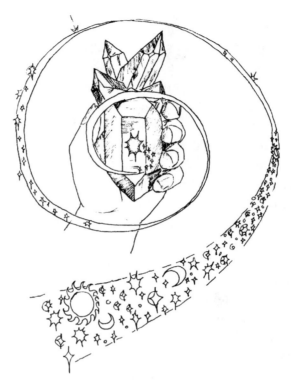

Aquarius' interest in other people and faraway places presents an ideal opportunity to visit a cultural or ethnic museum or festival. Check your community calendar to find out if any such events are being held in your area. While at the festivals or museums, find out what the people of the represented cultures do for fun, and what attitudes they have toward play. Try to learn something about their folklore and magical beliefs, then experiment with some of the simpler and more charming folk magic formulas for bringing luck.

Check to see whether you have a living history museum in your area, or an organization devoted to reconstructing past eras such as the Society for Creative Anachronism or other groups that stage recreations of historical events. Experience life in the past by viewing recreations of scenes, activities, and manners of bygone eras.

Along with this interest in the community of humanity comes an impulse for social activism. You might check to see if there's a political demonstration being staged somewhere, then go join in and show support for your side. Respect the Aquarian emphasis on reason by remaining peaceful and exercising self-control. Don't allow any of the mob energies to carry you away.

The Moon's transit through Aquarius stirs scientific curiosity, so some of this can be satisfied with a trip to a museum. Science museums which have interactive, hands-on exhibits are especially recommended. If you have the information and supplies available, set up some simple science experiments that can be performed at home. It's especially fun and educational if this experience can be shared with children. An important part of science is the recognition of the relationships of different principles, and the observations of children will surprise you with some of the new relationships they're capable of seeing.

Any artistic or inventive efforts are encouraged because the Moon in Aquarius accentuates the new and unusual and promotes innovative techniques and modes of creative expression. Utilize this energy by trying to be imaginative in whatever you do. Look for resourceful ways to approach work, cooking, household chores, etc. Have fun fooling around with gadgets, tools, and new technology.

Moon in Pisces

The Moon in Pisces brings subconscious knowledge closer to the surface and stimulates psychism. Go inward to learn the deep wisdom that is available when you practice meditation. This is an ideal time to visit a fortune teller or engage in psychic experimentation on your own. A lot of information is available on some simple forms of divination, like reading tea leaves or wax drippings. Record your dreams and intuitions. Consider whether there's anything in your dreams you can act out. By bringing something from the dream world into the waking world, you complete a circuit of energy.

Certain public places, such as historic homes, cemeteries, and other sites and buildings, are often said to have resident hauntings. The Moon's entry into Pisces enables you to be more sensitive to the spirit world, so make a little field trip to one of these places—provided you're not unnerved by this sort of thing.

Take advantage of tendencies toward escapism and fantasy by devoting yourself to artistic pursuits. You'll find it easier to bring your inner spiritual and romantic ideals of beauty into outward expression. Utilize the Piscean talent for imagination by trying some of the suggestions in Chapter 6, which is about infusing your world with fantasy. Rent some good science fiction, fantasy, or horror films or watch an imaginative television program, turning this escapist entertainment into a heart activity by snuggling up with your loved ones while you watch. Reading fairy tales, ghost

stories, and other folklore out loud to your family while you all sit around the hearth is another suggestion to create closeness.

Empathy for animals is greatly heightened when the Moon is in Pisces, so spend more time playing with and caring for the animals in your life. You might also go to a riding stable, farm, petting zoo, pet shop or show, or other place where you can interact with tame animals.

Experience Pisces' element directly—go to the beach. Try to sense the patterns of energy present in the action of waves and water. Listen for messages in the sounds of the moving water, as the ancient Teutonic priestesses used to do. Do some beach-combing to see what mysteries or treasures the ocean, lake, or river might choose to reveal on this day. Observe the activities of the people, birds, and animals who are found at the waterfront. If there's no beach near you, head for your nearest swimming pool or jacuzzi.

Endnotes

1. Llewellyn Publications, P.O. Box 64383, St. Paul, MN 55164-0383.

2. Scott Cunningham has written several excellent books on this subject, including *Magical Aromatherapy* (St. Paul: Llewellyn, 1989), and *The Complete Book of Incense, Oils and Brews* (St. Paul: Llewellyn, 1989).

3. There are a good number of books available. For a general overview of these topics, I recommend *All Women are Healers* by Diane Stein (Freedom: The Crossing Press, 1990). *Earth Mother Astrology* by Marcia Starck (St. Paul: Llewellyn, 1989) has a lot to say about how you can affect health and healing by using a wide variety of natural materials in harmony with astrological influences.

Afterword

The Yoga of Playfulness

The word "yoga" derives from the same root word as "yoke," and generally refers to different forms of self-monitored discipline. In our modern, highly pressured, highly structured society, allowing oneself the free time to do nothing obligatory, nothing programmed, but to just follow one's playful impulses can be the most difficult of all disciplines to follow. If you're sensitive to these pressures, or if you're an overly active person with a conscious mind that won't stop talking, even the simplest things (or what may like seem the simplest things to other people), may be a form of meditative discipline for you. Just try sitting, relaxing, and listening to a piece of music without trying to do something else at the same time, or thinking about other things. For such a person, this can be a difficult thing to do, but once you succeed, you'll find it is a profound experience.

If, like so many people, you've been denying yourself the right to have any personal interests for many years, the first few times you are able to designate some free time, you may not know what to do. If this is the case, light a candle and some incense, turn on some quiet, New Age, classical, or other instrumental music, then sit on the floor with your back to the wall. Quiet your mind and go into a semi-meditative state while asking yourself, "What do I want to do?" Relax and let impressions come to you. After a while, suggestions will come more spontaneously.

Consider getting up an hour earlier each day, so you can have one pure and unpolluted hour just to yourself. An hour of totally unstructured time. An hour to do anything you want. You can listen to music, go for invigorating walks, work crafts, read a book, meditate, even sit in a stupor and slowly sip on a cup of coffee. The only thing I would not recommend is watching TV. Other types of quiet activities help you connect with your inner Self, but TV chatter somehow seems inimical to that. But hey, the whole purpose of this is to kill time without guilt. So if watching TV is one of the things you've been denying yourself, or if you're one of those people who tries to do a dozen different chores while the TV is running, then just sitting down, paying attention, and watching a show from beginning to end can be a form of yoga. The important thing is to follow your instinct, trusting that your intuition will guide you to what's best for you.

Appendix I

The Use of Candles

A few of the magical workings and other activities in *Playful Magic* suggest or make reference to the use of candles. Candles are suggested for kicking off and wrapping up some of the spells, as well as for special purposes like the Thank-You candle.

Candle burning does more than create a certain ambience, it puts you in instant rapport with an elemental power, and has long been an important part of numerous mystical practices and folk magic traditions. The use of ritual and votive candles in many world's religions is itself a form of magic. The ancients viewed fire as a living creature which lends its vitality to any magical working. Because fire is synonymous with light, it symbolizes spiritual illumination and helps us tune into higher states of consciousness. Effective magical systems have been developed around the use of candles. Raymond Buckland's book *Practical Candle Burning Rituals* and Kala and Ketz Pajeon's *Candle Magick Workbook* are good sources for anyone wishing to look deeper into this practice.

Practitioners of candle magic generally "dress" the candles with scented oils to dedicate them, boosting their energy, and sharpening their focus. To dress a candle, just pour a little oil on your fingertips, then rub them over the candle, starting at about the middle and working outward to both ends. As you anoint the candle, think about the magical goal you're working on. Complete the dressing by covering the wick and the bottom of the candle.

Scented oils can be obtained in craft shops, florists, candle shops, import shops, and occult and New Age shops. Any scent that appeals to you will be suitable. If you wish to be more particular, occult shops and catalogs sell specialty oils meant for use with love spells, money spells, and others. Consult Scott Cunningham's *The Complete Book of Incense, Oils and Brews* for more information on the magical connotations of different scents.

The size, shape, and type of candle isn't important. Use whatever is handy. In the course of experimenting with some playfully magical suggestions, you may be able to find a use for some of those odd-shaped candles you may have around your home.

To choose candles in colors appropriate for the mood you'd like to create or the things you'd like to achieve, see Appendix II. Burn the candles for a specified amount of time, in conjunction with whatever other magical work you are doing. Put the candles out when you're through and reuse them later.

Appendix II

The Use of Colors

In trying out some of the magical suggestions, spells and techniques in *Playful Magic,* you may want to use color symbolism in your choice of candles, flowers, crafts materials, or decor. Following is a list of the traditional magical and psychological correspondences of colors.

Black: Total concentration, impenetrability, protection, immovability, firm and somber resolve, absence of light.

Black and White: The Cabalistic colors of knowledge, black represents understanding because it absorbs all light, white represents the quintessence of Divine Light.

Blue: Depth of emotion, peace, serenity, relaxation, honesty, fidelity, truth, kindness, the color of philosophy faculties in American colleges.

Blue, dark: Understanding, introspection, concentration, patience, the contractive (inward directed) aspect of intellect.

Blue, light: Peace in the home, sincerity, loyalty, empathy, devotion, gentility, delicate charm, gracefulness.

Blue-green: Emotional soothing, healing and nourishment, the healing power of art, mystical unity with Nature, regeneration, intuitive vision.

Blue-violet, Indigo: Spiritual reflection, meditation, intuition, going deep within.

Brown: Pride in simple ways, love of simple pleasures found in living close to the Earth, Earth powers, strength rooted in the Earth, stability, supportiveness, the security and emotional riches of home and hearth.

Gold: Personal pride and self-confidence, radiance, charisma, attractiveness, expansiveness, creative activity, success, initiative, leadership, power, authority, prosperity, luck.

Green: Living Nature, the freedom of Wilderness, youth, growth, fertility, resilience, adaptation, regeneration, bodily healing, color of medical faculties in American colleges, opportunity, prosperity, money, financial security, comfort, the Druidic color of knowledge.

Orange: Warmth, high energy, vitality, focused energy, self motivation, free expression, boldness, action directed by intellect, unity of mind and body (combining thought, will, and action), persuasion, endurance. This is the color assigned to engineering faculties in American colleges.

Orange-red: Assertiveness, activity, competitiveness, enthusiasm, wildness, force of will.

Mauve: Qualities of pink, but more retiring; desire subtlety, dignity.

Peach: Warmth and softness, social harmony (it makes people feel safe and assured, enables people to connect with each other); the softness of pink, with the enthusiasm and energy of orange.

Pink, rose: Affection, loving, nurturing, warm feelings, feeling good, well-being, pride in femininity, pleasure in self; everything looks better in the glow of pink or peach; color assigned to music faculties in American colleges.

Purple, violet: Altered states of consciousness, spirituality, psychism, inspiration, dynamic creativity (combines intuition with action), love of drama, dignity, focused power, authority, high status in life, nobility, generosity, appreciation of variety, tolerance for differences; color worn by law faculties in American colleges.

Red: Energy, vital force, enthusiasm, activity, impulse, immediate action, human love, desire, passion, sexuality, eroticism, conception, childbearing and childbirth.

Red, dark: Sensitivity combined with the active and sensual qualities of red; a craving for the riches of life; love of power, wealth, and position.

Red-violet: Ambition, noble actions, adds passion to the spiritual and mystical nature.

Silver: Subtle lunar energies, ethereal beauty, romantic feelings, mysterious charm, mystique, purity of understanding, the receptive aspects of creativity, clarity, purity, integrity, honesty, self-worth, idealism.

White: Purification, purity of intentions, innocence of spirit, psychic energy, spiritual strength, purified emotions, absence of negative feeling, unity and harmony (because white is all the colors in the spectrum combined).

Yellow: Brightness, happiness, cheer, hopefulness, expectations, intellect, alertness, wit, wisdom, science, confidence, spontaneity, enjoyment of action, communication, questing for alternative experience; the active (outward directed) aspect of intelligence.

Yellow-green: The calming and centered qualities of green, with more emphasis on intellect and activity; cool, with the confidence and love of challenges of yellow.

Appendix III

Magical
Symbolism

Some of the magical and meditational suggestions and projects in this book can be enhanced by a knowledge of symbolism. Meaningful images can be incorporated into some of the craft projects done with magical intent. Toys, miniatures, and collectibles can be symbolic objects, as well as many of the things you might bring into your house for workings the Good Things Coming In spell. There are also a lot of things you can do with small charms and objects used in jewelry, crafts such as the Tree of Life collage and the like. When you draw or craft these symbols, or have them in your home or wear them, you are materially affirming, "I already possess this thing or this quality. It is already so."

In the following list and in other books that explore the meaning of symbols, interpretations are drawn from a variety of sources, including psychological approaches like Jungian or Freudian, world philosophical traditions, religions, folk magic, and the intuition and experience of the authors in dealing with psychology, magic, and magic workers. The magical use of symbols can be pretty straight-forward, such as hearts to attract love, ballet shoes for a dancer, or personal zodiac signs to help the wearer connect with this part of his/her nature. Even when the meanings aren't apparent on the surface, there's always some sort of logic involved—although not all the systems used to explain symbolism may be of use or relevance to you as an individual.

Symbols are highly personal in nature, so naturally the same creature, object, dream image, or event can mean different things to different people. When we perceive things as symbols, we are making associations based on our own mindset and experience, and projecting our own meanings into them. (We should always bear in mind that these objects or creatures have existence, purpose, and uniqueness independent of the meanings we ascribe to them.) If you're attracted to a certain symbol, then it's as though it's speaking to you. You need to ask yourself what sort of associations come to mind, what the message could be, then allow your intuition to give the answer. Usually, the first impression you get is going to be the most accurate interpretation to you personally.

Most symbols are quite complex, have many possible meanings, and can be interpreted on several levels. The interpretations given in the following lists are necessarily short, generalized, simple, and of a lighter nature. The designs chosen for use here are ones that are more familiar, that you would be most likely to use in simple crafts projects, and that are more readily available in the form of charms and the like. Use these lists as guidelines, but if certain interpretations don't ring true to you, then go by the feelings that these symbols awaken in you.

Geometrics

Circle: Eternity, completion, fulfillment, wholeness, the Self, spirituality, the spiritual world, oneness with the Cosmos, the perfection of Zen.

Chain: Continuity of life with past, present, and future; the inter-relatedness of all living.

Cross: Protection (through the shielding action of the four elements); also the union of elements and opposites.

Cross Surmounted by Circle (Ankh): Physical life in harmony with spiritual life.

Cross Within a Circle (Celtic Cross): The Earth and her four quarters; the union of Earth with the spiritual world.

Figure 8: Eternity, the dynamic balance of solar and lunar forces.

Square: Stability, the foundation of the home, the material world and material security.

Spiral: Evolution, growth and progress, the flow of energy through space, landforms, and living things.

Star, 5-Pointed (Pentagram): the energy generated when the four elements are bound together with the fifth element, spirit; humanity as the manifestation of this synergy and a microcosm of the perfection of the Living Universe.

Star, 6-Pointed (Star of David): Union of opposites and harmonious balance of creative forces make this the Star of Creation.

Triangle: Creative focus of body, mind, and spirit; the triad of energy, matter, and space; the active power of the fire element when pointing upward, the nourishing power of water when inverted; the inverted triangle is also a widespread paleolithic art motif symbolizing the regenerative power of the Mother Goddess.

Animal Symbolism

Bat: Asian charm depicts five bats as the blessings of health, wealth, love of virtue, old age, and a natural death.

Bear: Childbearing, powerfully protective mother instincts (teddy bears for bear hugs, nurturing qualities of mama bears), hibernation symbolizes introspection and self-renewal.

Bees, Beetles, Winged Insects: Harbingers of Spring, Earth's fertility, social cooperation, industriousness.

Butterfly: Ancient symbol of the soul, exemplifies transformation; represents an early and happy marriage in some Asian cultures.

Cat: Personal pride, self-assurance, love of beauty and comfort; in magic, black cats are especially lucky (associations with bad luck come from the Medieval Church, which reviled cats because they were the totem animals of the Love Goddess); embody "the Spirit of Place" because of their attachment to their homes.

Cow: Earth mother, nourishment, taking care of physical needs, the wealth of the Earth, fertility cycles of the Moon.

Coyote: Cleverness, guise of the trickster, surviving by one's wits.

Deer: Maternal affection, healing touch, grace and gentility.

Dog: Companionship, fidelity, household guardian.

Dolphin: The connection between human sentience and that of the animal kingdom.

Dragon: The raw, powerful, flowing energies of the Life Force as it courses through landforms and the elements of Fire, Water, and Air.

Dragonfly: Ethereal, illusory beauty; popular Art Nouveau motif.

Fish: The Water element, fertility and richness.

Frog: Transformation, evolution, small impulses that lead to meaningful things; also, the herald of nourishing rain and the beginning of Spring.

Horse: Great power coupled with great gentility, personal power in both physical and spiritual domains.

Ladybug: Good luck coming from the gifts of the Love Goddess.

Lamb: Innocence, the playful vitality of youth.

Lion: The raw power of the Fire element.

Lizard: Basking habits show the lizard's love of the Sun, and the Sun returns that love; symbolizes the solar powers that value and nourish even the small things.

Mouse: The importance of the small things in life. (With Aesop's maxim in mind: "Look to the small things, and the big things will take care of themselves.")

Pig: Their rounded shapes suggest pregnancy, fertility, and abundance, their rooting around also associates them with the Earth mysteries.

Rabbit: Fertility, sexuality, abundance.

Scarab Beetle: Transformation, rebirth into eternal life.

Serpent: Associated with the healing arts because of self-renewal and spiralling coils suggesting the flow of the Life Force; and going into the ground represents knowledge of the mysteries.

Spider: The web of life (ancient symbol relevant to modern ecology), personal skill, good luck for craftspersons and witches.

Toad: A spirit of place that confers well being to a home; recognizing beauty in homely things (the word "homely" once referred to the ability to create a comfortable home).

Turtle: Longevity and protective security; in Native American lore, the foundation of the Earth.

Unicorn: Purity, innocence, justice, the untouched state of Nature.

Wolf: Finding new energy by making contact with the inner, wild, and primitive level of being.

Bird Symbolism

Birds, general: Thought, imagination, intuition, freedom, transcendence, spiritual help for inspiration, speed toward your goals; birds are the messengers of the gods and an omen that the Living Universe wants you to know your quest has meaning.

Birds, water : Associated with abundance, fertility, and transformation as far back as the paleolithic era.

Chicken: Security and prosperity of a cozy homestead.

Dove: Peace, love, and fertility, as well as a symbol that reminds us that all life is infused with spirit.

Duck: The term, "as a duck takes to water," refers to finding your own element and doing what comes naturally; a symbol of being yourself, following your instinct, finding your right path or place.

Eagle: Spiritual power, the ability to soar beyond all limitations.

Hawks: Alertness, awareness, ability to see the heart of a matter.

Hummingbird: Pure joy, ecstatic lightness of being, love charm.

Owl: Wisdom, knowledge; go-betweens 'twixt night and day, life and death, the Middle Earth and Otherworld.

Parrot: A love for exotic places, communication, and sociability.

Peacock: Personal pride, love of beauty.

Rooster: Courage; the victory of light over darkness.

Sea Gull: Ability to travel through many dimensions as gulls are at home in three elements: Earth, Air, and Water; an appropriate symbol for the shaman.

Stork: Believed to bring babies because it is an ancient symbol of incipient life (see *Birds, water*); symbolizes good parenting and a reciprocal devotion to one's own parents.

Swallow: Bird that best embodies the playful Spirit of Air, a harbinger of Spring, traditionally a good luck amulet.

Swan: Feminine grace and beauty that stirs Divine inspiration.

inner conflict about his worthiness to lead; displays the stable and conscientious qualities of the Earth element.

The Little Mermaid: The playful, inquisitive aspects of the archetypal Maiden, drawing energy from the Elemental World (especially as portrayed in the recent Disney character, Ariel).

Mario: The take-action type of person who shoulders the responsibility for saving and maintaining the world; certain types of codependents may be able to identify with Mario.

Michaelangelo: A laid-back Ninja turtle, a no problem, party-on kind of dude; has the easy-going qualities of the Water element.

Mickey Mouse: The average guy, doing his best; the typical young, single American male who enjoys his friends and looks forward to dates with his girlfriend on weekends.

Minnie Mouse: A classical anima figure, the idealized feminine, the dream woman.

Peter Pan: The inner child, that archetypal energy that will not be confined or limited, an emanation of the great god Pan.

Porky the Pig: He's good natured and his friends accept him; he misses a lot of the things that go by; if this is a totem for you, it could signify your recognition that you have to bring yourself more in tune with the objective world.

Princess Toadstool: Anima figure; she serves to inspire adventurers and serve as a figurehead for her people.

Raphael: The hot-headed Ninja turtle who likes to break off on his own, represents the spiky qualities of elemental Fire.

Roadrunner: The free spirit who experiences the thrill of challenge and the joy of the open road.

Rocky the Squirrel: The voice of common sense, but likes flying, traveling, and adventure.

Scrooge McDuck: Boot-straps, self-made capitalist who knows how to handle money, but is on the verge of realizing that there's more to life.

The Simpsons: A reaction to the idealized TV families who are so wise, loving, and supportive. The Simpson characters can stand for letting go of blame by acknowledging your family's flaws (the problem with all this talk of dysfunctional families is that it implies that somewhere there exists a functional family).

Snow White: Archetypal Kore figure; like the maiden who tames the unicorn, her beauty and purity acts as a catalyst to make major things happen.

Splinter: The Zen master who is the Ninja Turtles' mentor; he's like the fifth point on the pentagram, the spiritual element that binds the other four elements together.

Wile E. Coyote: Perseverance, despite the constant failure of his outrageous schemes (interestingly enough, the Native American trickster figure, known as Coyote, Manabozho, and by many other names, suffered similar set-backs).

Appendix IV

Affirmations

The use of affirmations is a practice which has become an important part of many popular therapies, as well as spiritual and metaphysical disciplines. When a person writes or recites an affirmation, she or he is essentially making a positive statement about a quality, desire, goal, or thing that she or he would like to reinforce or bring into reality. These statements are always framed in a way to affirm that the desired thing already exists.

Psychology uses affirmations as a tool for self-improvement because they help persons focus on their goals. The metaphysical theory behind affirmations is that there is a creative force in the universe which aligns itself with our own thoughts and attitudes and brings them into reality. This force does not judge or evaluate our beliefs, it merely mirrors them in the world around us. According to the theory, negative beliefs such as, "I don't have enough money," will contribute to making poverty a continuing situation, while positive thoughts such as, "I'm a very lucky person," will create a state of serendipity. Such affirmations call on you to trust your Deity, the Living Universe, the Cosmos, the Universal Intelligence, the Divine Process, the Process of Life, or whatever name you ascribe the creative force that animates and informs the Universe.

Affirmations are always worded in the present tense. You would say, "I am healed," or "I am healing," rather than, "I will be healed." When you affirm things you want, you try to avoid wording them in the future tense, because that could keep them always in the future.

Sometimes repeating a statement like, "I have lots of money," may sound like you're telling yourself an outrageous lie, so you have to put yourself in a different frame of mind—what I describe as a magical frame of mind. For persons who feel funny about saying affirmations that seem too unrealistic, there's a suggestion for creating a "Wishing Place" in Chapter 6, a special place where you can accept that you're stepping into a magical reality, where you can feel that when wishes are made in this place, anything can happen.

I have noticed one problem with the trend for saying affirmations (other than whipping yourself into a frenzy of positive thinking and then wondering why you haven't won the lottery), and that is becoming obsessive-compulsive about them. I knew one lady who was in some kind of a recovery program that required her to write down a hundred affirmations each morning. Trying to find the time to do this left her really frazzled, which kind of defeated the purpose. Therefore, if you choose to do any affirmations to help develop a playful attitude and cultivate the art of playful magic, use them only as long as it's pleasurable to do so, don't let the saying of affirmations become an obligatory chore.

Following are a few playful affirmations to create a favorable mood for cheerfulness, spontaneity, creativity, and other playful qualities:

Enjoying Life

I celebrate pleasure,
  and open myself to pleasure.
I take pleasure in my body, and in my self.
I take pleasure in being me.
I revel in the flow of life.
I celebrate every life around me.
I am one with the pulse of Creation.
Success is the natural expression
  of my enjoyment of life.
My day is filled with pleasurable activity,
  and I make my work my pleasure.

Sunshine and Happiness

I embrace joy, I welcome happiness,
  and cheerfulness fills me with radiance.
I greet my day with joy,
  as I greet the golden sun,
   and the glowing sun within me.
I'm riding a wave of golden sunlight.
The sunlight warms me,
  and shines through me.
Sunlight flows into every far corner
  of life and being.

High Energy

I am alive with energy and vitality,
The Life Force is a bright fire within me.
It fills me with lightness.
It fills me with exhilaration.
I am at one with the dance of life,
  and all life flows through me.

Spontaneity and Taking
Life as It Comes

My world is filled with creative opportunities.
I welcome each adventure that comes my way.
I enjoy the day to its fullest,
*   and meet every challenge with enthusiasm.*
I welcome every challenge
*   as an opportunity to exercise my creativity.*
I approach new problems creatively,
*   and dismiss old guilt with a sense of humor.*
I experience the ebb and the flow, I allow life to happen.

The Magical Life

My life is suffused with magic.
I live in a world of enchantment.
I am a part of a greater world of wonder.
Every moment carries rewards,
Every moment carries enchantments.
This is a day of magic, a day of wonder,
*   a day when anything is possible!*

Luck

All channels of good are open to me.
Luck comes to me in unexpected ways,
*   and unexpected places.*
I have the golden touch,
*   and everything that touches me is golden.*
I receive golden gifts,
*   for I am Lady Fortune's child.*

Note: The affirmations that accompany Chapter 5 can also be used for general purposes.

 *Bibliography*

The following books, which have been quoted or referred to in *Playful Magic,* represent a wide and seemingly disparate selection of subjects, but they all touch on the subject of bringing magic into everyday life.

Bach, Marcus. *The Wonderful Magic of Living. The World of Serendipity.* Marina Del Ray: DeVorss, 1970.

Bolen, Jean. *The Tao of Psychology.* San Francisco: Harper and Row, 1979.

Brown, Tom. *Tom Brown's Field Guide to Nature Observation and Tracking.* New York: Berkley Books, 1983.

Brown, Tom. *The Vision.* New York: Berkley Books, 1988.

Campanelli, Pauline. *Wheel of the Year, Living the Magical Life.* St. Paul: Llewellyn, 1989.

Campbell, Joseph. *The Flight of the Wild Gander.* Washington D.C.: Gateway, 1951.

Castaneda, Carlos. *The Teachings of Don Juan: A Yaqui Way of Knowledge.* New York: Simon and Schuster. 1968.

Combs, Allan, and Holland, Mark. *Synchronicity—Science, Myth, and the Trickster.* New York: Paragon House, 1990.

Corbett, Cynthia L., Ph.D. *Power Trips, Journeys to Sacred Sites as a Way of Transformation.* Santa Fe: Timewindow Publications, 1988.

Cunningham, Scott. *Magical Aromatherapy.* St. Paul: Llewellyn, 1989.

Cunningham, Scott. *The Complete Book of Incense, Oils and Brews.* St. Paul: Llewellyn, 1989.

Dittman, Margaret. *The Fabric Lover's Scrapbook.* Radnor: Chilton, 1988.

Erikson, Joan Mowat. *The Universal Bead.* New York: Norton, 1969.

Fitch, Ed. *Magical Rites from the Crystal Well.* St. Paul: Llewellyn, 1984.

The Green Egg. Ukiah: POB 1542.

Hay, Louise L. *You Can Heal Your Life.* Santa Monica: Hay House, 1984.

Hillman, James. *Lectures on Jung's Typology: The Feeling Function.* Dallas: Spring Publications, 1971.

Howell, Alice O. *The Dove in the Stone, Finding the Sacred in the Commonplace.* Wheaton: Theosophical Publishing House, 1988.

Jeffries, William C. *True to Type.* Norfolk: Hampton Roads Publishing, 1991.

Judith, Anodea. *The Truth about Chakras.* St. Paul: Llewellyn, 1990.

Judith, Anodea. *Wheels of Life.* St. Paul: Llewellyn, 1990.

Keirsey, David, and Bates, Marilyn. *Please Understand Me: Character and Temperament Types.* Del Mar: Prometheus Nemesis Book Company, 1984.

Lawlor, Robert. *Voices of the First Day: Awakening in the Aboriginal Dreamtime.* Rochester: Inner Traditions, 1991.

Leopold, Aldo. *A Sand County Almanac.* New York: Ballantine, 1984, originally 1949.

Llewellyn's Moon Sign Book. St. Paul: Llewellyn, annual pub.

Maclaine, Shirley. *Going Within, A Guide for Inner Transformation.* New York: Bantam, 1989.

Michell, John. *The Earth Spirit, Its Ways, Shrines, and Mysteries.* New York: Thames and Hudson, 1975.

Pajeon, Kala and Katz. *The Candle Magic Workbook.* New York: Carol Publishing Group, 1991.

Pearsall, Paul, Ph.D. *Super Joy.* New York: Doubleday, 1988.

Pennick, Nigel. *Games of the Gods.* York Beach: Weiser, 1989.

Renee, Janina. *Tarot Spells.* St. Paul: Llewellyn, 1990.

Sherwood, Keith. *Chakra Therapy for Personal Growth and Healing.* St. Paul: Llewellyn, 1989.

Skinner, Charles M. *Myths and Legends of FLowers, Trees, Fruits, and Plants.* Philadelphia: Lippincott, 1911.

Sun Bear. *Honoring Sacred Places,* from Lehrman, Frederic, ed., *The Sacred Landscape.* Berkely: Celestial Arts, 1988.

Swan, James A. *Sacred Places, How the Living Earth Seeks Our Friendship.* Santa Fe: Bear and Co., 1990.

Swan, James A. *The Power of Place, Sacred Ground in Natural and Human Environments.* Wheaton: Theosophical Publishing House, 1991.

Starck, Marcia. *Earth Mother Astrology.* St. Paul: Llewellyn, 1989.

Starhawk. *The Spiral Dance.* San Francisco: Harper and Row, 1979.

Stein, Diane. *All Women are Healers.* Freedom: The Crossing Press, 1990.

Sui, Choa Kok. *Pranic Healing.* York Beach: Weiser, 1987.

von Franz, Marie-Louise. *Lectures on Jung's Typology: The Inferior Function.* Dallas: Spring Publications, 1971.

Walker, Barbara. *Women's Rituals.* San Francisco: Harper and Row, 1990.

Wolfe, Amber. *In the Shadow of the Shaman.* St. Paul: Llewellyn, 1988.

Stay in Touch

On the following pages you will find some of the books now available on related subjects. Your book dealer stocks most of these and will stock new Llewellyn titles as they become available.

To obtain our full catalog, to keep informed about new titles as they are released and to benefit from informative articles and helpful news, you are invited to write for our bimonthly news magazine/catalog, *Llewellyn's New Worlds of Mind and Spirit*. A sample copy is free, and it will continue coming to you at no cost as long as you are an active mail customer. Or you may subscribe for just $10.00 in the U.S.A. and Canada ($20.00 overseas, first class mail). Many bookstores also have New Worlds available to their customers. Ask for it.

Llewellyn's New Worlds of Mind and Spirit
P.O. Box 64383-678, St. Paul, MN 55164-0383, U.S.A.

To Order Books and Tapes

If your book dealer does not have the books described, you may order them directly from the publisher by sending the full price in U.S. funds, plus $3.00 for postage and handling for orders under $10.00; $4.00 for orders over $10.00. There are no postage and handling charges for orders over $50.00. Postage and handling rates are subject to change. We ship UPS whenever possible. Delivery guaranteed. Provide your street address as UPS does not deliver to P.O. Boxes. UPS to Canada requires a $50.00 minimum order. Allow 4-6 weeks for delivery. Orders outside the U.S.A. and Canada: Airmail—add retail price of book; add $5.00 for each non-book item (tapes, etc.); add $1.00 per item for surface mail.

For Group Study and Purchase

Because there is a great deal of interest in group discussion and study of the subject matter of this book, we offer a special quantity price to group leaders or agents. Our Special Quantity Price for a minimum order of five copies of *Playful Magic* is $38.85 cash-with-order. This price includes postage and handling within the United States. Minnesota residents must add 6.5% sales tax. For additional quantities, please order in multiples of five. For Canadian and foreign orders, add postage and handling charges as above. Credit card (VISA, MasterCard, American Express) orders are accepted. Charge card orders only ($15.00 minimum order) may be phoned in free within the U.S.A. or Canada by dialing 1-800-THE-MOON. For customer service, call 1-612-291-1970. Mail orders to:

LLEWELLYN PUBLICATIONS
P.O. Box 64383-678, St. Paul, MN 55164-0383, U.S.A.

TAROT SPELLS
by Janina Renee

Tarot Spells provides a means of recognizing and affirming one's own personal power through use of the Tarot. With the practical advice and beautiful illustrations in this book, the reader can perform spells for: influencing dreams, improving health, better family relations, beating addiction, finding a job, better gardening, and more. Thirty-five areas of life are discussed, along with spells which address specific issues in these areas.

The reader uses Tarot layouts in combination with affirmations and visualizations to obtain a desired result. Many spells can be used with color, gemstones, or magical tools to assist the reader in focusing his or her desire.

Graced with beautiful card illustrations from the Robin Wood Tarot, *Tarot Spells* can be used immediately even by those who don't own a Tarot deck. No previous experience with the Tarot is necessary. Those familiar with the Tarot can gain new insights into the symbolism of their own particular deck.

0-87542-670-0, 288 pgs., 6 x 9, illus., softcover   **$12.95**

WITCHCRAFT TODAY, BOOK THREE:
Witchcraft and Shamanism
edited by Chas S. Clifton

Witchcraft Today, Book Three is a compelling and honest examination of shamanic techniques (both classical and neoclassical) as they are being practiced in neopagan Witchcraft in the 1990s. Shamanism is a natural adjunct to the ritualistic and magical practice of many covens and solitary Pagans. In this groundbreaking volume, you will discover how others have integrated techniques such as trance journeys, soul retrieval, and altered states of consciousness.

Discover how shamanic ideas influenced Greek philosophers, Platonists, Pythagoreans, and Gnostics... learn how evidence from the old witch trials suggests that at least some Europeans may have practiced shamanic journeying in the past... incorporate caves for ritual and inner journeys, both literally and in visualization... find out who is retrieving souls and curing elfshot... compare the guided visualizations common to modern magickal practice with the neoshamanic journey... learn how spirit contacts are made, how guides are perceived, and in what "worlds" they reside... and much more.

1-56718-150-3, 304 pgs., 5¼ x 8, photos, softcover   **$9.95**